BrightRED Study Guide

CfE HIGHER

DRAMA

Kerry Reith

First published in 2017 by:
Bright Red Publishing Ltd
1 Torphichen Street
Edinburgh
EH3 8HX

A CIP record for this book is available from the British Library.

ISBN 978-1-906736-84-2

With thanks to:
PDQ Digital Media Solutions Ltd, Bungay (layout), Susan Milligan (copy-edit).

Cover design and series book design by Caleb Rutherford – e i d e t i c.

Acknowledgements
Every effort has been made to seek all copyright-holders. If any have been overlooked, then Bright Red Publishing will be delighted to make the necessary arrangements.

Permission has been sought from all relevant copyright holders and Bright Red Publishing are grateful for the use of the following:

Images from Ingram Image on pages 7, 11, 12, 14, 15, 32, 37, 39, 42, 47, 48, 51, 80, 82, 85, 88 and 89; Caleb Rutherford, e i d e t i c (p 6); AlexanderMas/iStock.com (p 7); Kurt Magoon (CC BY-SA 2.0)[1] (p 8); MariaBrzostowska/iStock.com (p 8); An illustration from 'The Moon Belongs to Everyone: Making Theatre with 7:84' by Elizabeth MacLennan (Methuen 1990). Reproduced by permission of Methuen Drama, an imprint of Bloomsbury Publishing (p 9); An image from 'Black Watch' - The National Theatre of Scotland, photography by Manuel Harlan (p 10); An image from 'The Curious Incident of the Dog in the Night-Time' – National Theatre, photography by Brinkhoff/Mögenburg (p 10); An extract from The Curious Incident of the Dog in the Night-Time by Mark Haddon (Jonathan Cape, 2003) © Mark Haddon (2003) (p 13); IPGGutenbergUKLtd /iStock.com (p 16); briefshots/iStock.com (p 18); Lonely_/iStock.com (p 19); Steven Pisano (CC BY 2.0)[2] (p 20); Hernán Piñera (CC BY-SA 2.0)[1] (p 21); Samantha MacDonald (p 22); Michael Pollak (CC BY 2.0)[2] (p 23); Flavio~ (CC BY 2.0)[2] (p 24); U.S. Embassy Tel Aviv (CC BY-ND 2.0)[3] (pp 24 & 25); Becoming An Actor (CC BY-SA 2.0)[1] (p 26); University of the Fraser Valley (CC BY 2.0)[2] (p 26); Joe Futrelle (CC BY-SA 2.0)[1] (p 26); jackfoto/iStock.com (p 29); Jason Scragz (CC BY 2.0)[2] (p 30); Steven Depolo (CC BY 2.0)[2] (p 31); Joe Hart (CC BY 2.0)[2] (p 31); An adaptation from 'Respect for Acting' by Uta Hagen (New York: Wiley Publishing, Inc.) © Uta Hagen (1973) (p 33); Becoming An Actor (CC BY-SA 2.0)[1] (p 34); shvili/iStock.com (p 35); Dslaven/Dreamstime.com (p 36); Becoming An Actor (CC BY-SA 2.0)[1] (p 38); University of the Fraser Valley (CC BY 2.0)[2] (p 40); Steven Pisano (CC BY 2.0)[2] (p 41); foam (CC BY-SA 2.0)[1] (p 43); christopher.durant (CC BY 2.0)[2] (p 44); Eva Rinaldi (CC BY-SA 2.0)[1] (p 46); Alfredo Cofré (CC BY-SA 2.0)[1] (p 52); aka Tman (CC BY 2.0)[2] (p 53); dlritter/FreeImages.com (p 54); no credit for this image?? (p 55); Vancouver Film School (CC BY 2.0)[2] (p 56); Henning Halfpap (CC BY-SA 2.0)[1] (p 57); Zsuzsa N.K./FreeImages.com (p 59); An extract from 'The House of Bernarda Alba' by Federico García Lorca (public domain) (p 59); Nazareth College (CC BY 2.0)[2] (p 60); An extract from 'The Prime of Miss Jean Brodie' by Muriel Spark (London: Macmillan & Co.) © Muriel Spark (1961) (p 60); An extract from 'Lovers' by Brian Friel (New York: Farrar, Straus & Giroux) © Brian Friel (1968) (p 61); An extract from 'A Taste of Honey' by Shelagh Delaney (London: Methuen & Co.) © Shelagh Delaney (1959) (p 61); Image from 'A Taste of Honey' by Shelagh Delaney, featuring Traci Asaurus and Maynard Okereke, at Eclectic Theater © Scott Maddock (p 61); University of the Fraser Valley (CC BY 2.0)[2] (p 62); MiraCosta Community College (Public Domain) (p 64); Hans Splinter (CC BY-ND 2.0)[3] (p 65); An image from 'Kill Johnny Glendenning' by DC Jackson, a co-production between the Royal Lyceum Theatre Edinburgh and Citizens Theatre, photography by Robbie Jack (p 66); An image from 'Dunsinane' – The National Theatre of Scotland, photography by Richard Campbell (p 68); Filipe Saraiva (CC BY 2.0)[2] (p 70); Virginia Tech School of Performing Arts (CC BY-ND 2.0)[3] (p 72); Caleb Rutherford, e i d e t i c (p 74); Elle Marci (CC BY 2.0)[2] (p 76); Extracts from 'The Crucible' by Arthur Miller (New York: Dramatists Play Service Inc.) © Arthur Miller (1953) (pp 76–77); Virginia Tech School of Performing Arts (CC BY-ND 2.0)[3] (p 86); Sasha Kargaltsev (CC BY 2.0)[2] (p 86).

[1] (CC BY-SA 2.0) http://creativecommons.org/licenses/by-sa/2.0/
[2] (CC BY 2.0) http://creativecommons.org/licenses/by/2.0/
[3] (CC BY-ND 2.0) https://creativecommons.org/licenses/by-nd/2.0/

Printed and bound in the UK by Martins the Printers.

CONTENTS

INTRODUCTION

STUDYING CfE HIGHER DRAMA

Higher Drama is a challenging but rewarding course. It offers the opportunity to develop and deepen skills in creating, performing and analysing drama. Through both the Drama Skills and Production Skills units, you will develop a range of skills that will benefit you in the final exam and beyond. You will gain new skills and abilities through creating and performing drama. You will also develop knowledge and understanding of cultural and social influences on drama. In addition, you will analyse the effectiveness of your own creative work, as well as that of your peers and professional theatre productions.

You will study and analyse a chosen text throughout the course. You will analyse and understand this text from three different perspectives: as an actor, a director and a designer. It is also a requirement of the course that you analyse professional theatre productions and you should seek out opportunities to attend as many, and as wide a range of, theatre productions as you can. You can also watch live recordings of theatrical productions through Digital Theatre and NT Live. Being exposed to as much theatre as possible will greatly enhance your performance in all areas of the course.

DRAMA SKILLS

In this unit of the course, you will develop your creative skills to devise and direct an original theatrical production from a given **stimulus** or text. You will also perform in productions devised by your peers and you will be assessed on your acting skills. **Experimentation** is encouraged and it is essential that you are able to work as part of a team while still taking responsibility for your own development.

PRODUCTION SKILLS

In the Production Skills unit, you will **develop** your abilities in at least two of the three areas of acting, directing and design. You will look at how the production team work together to create a **performance**, and you will gain a deep understanding of the different roles, developing your talents in at least two of these areas. You will work as part of a team, but also have individual responsibility for the direction and/or acting and/or designing of an extract from a text.

EVALUATION

Within both of the course components, you will undertake an evaluation of your own and your peers' performance. Through this evaluation, you will develop analysis skills and reflect on your performance in order to improve in the future. You will also reflect on the work of others and analyse how they could improve their performance.

TEXTUAL ANALYSIS

Throughout the course, you will study a chosen text. You will explore its context, themes and issues and undertake research into the play. This will help you to develop your understanding and ability to act in, direct and design the play for a contemporary **audience**.

PERFORMANCE ANALYSIS

Throughout the course you will undertake in-depth analysis of professional theatre productions. You will look at the different aspects of the performance and how they communicate with the audience.

COURSE ASSESSMENT: PERFORMANCE

As part of the final assessment of the course, you will undertake a practical exam, either as an actor, director or designer. The practical exam is worth 50 marks, with an additional Preparation for Performance (PfP) which is worth 10 marks. The requirements of the practical exam differ depending on which role you decide to undertake.

As an actor, you will perform **two characters**. Each performance is a maximum of ten minutes in length. You will be assessed on your ability to utilise **voice** and **movement** skills, demonstrate **characterisation** and on the overall impact on the audience.

As a director, you will prepare to direct a substantial section from your chosen text, for example an act. On the day of the exam, the visiting assessor (VA) will ask you to prepare a **rehearsal** for a short extract of around two pages from your chosen section. You will then lead a rehearsal for the extract and answer any questions from the VA. You will be assessed on your interaction with your actors, your interpretation and your **performance concepts**. The rehearsal will last around 30 minutes.

As a designer, you will design a set for your chosen text. You will also choose one additional production role from lighting, sound, costume, props, make-up and hair. You will present your designs to the VA on the assessment day, in addition to demonstrating how your design will be used in performance. The presentation will last around 20 minutes.

Preparation for Performance

This section of the practical exam is worth 10 marks. It is not a folio; it is a summation of how you have interpreted and developed your chosen role. It should include details of:

- how you researched your text(s) and role
- your interpretation of the chosen role
- how you developed the role for performance.

The VA will mark this before your performance/presentation.

COURSE ASSESSMENT: THE WRITTEN PAPER

The written exam is split into two sections. In Section One you will write an essay from the perspective of an actor, or a director, or a designer. This essay will allow you to analyse your chosen text and explain how your production will **communicate** your understanding of the text. In Section Two you will analyse a contemporary theatre performance. To form this in-depth analysis, you will **focus** on TWO key production areas from a choice of four and discuss how these areas **contribute** to the impact on the audience.

 **DON'T FORGET**

Design includes set, costume, props, lighting, sound, make-up and hair.

DRAMA SKILLS

THE DRAMA PROCESS

In this chapter, we will explore the requirements of the Drama Skills unit of Higher Drama. We will look at possible ways of approaching and structuring your work throughout the unit, in addition to exploring stimuli and possible influences on your work.

This unit will develop your ability to create and perform original drama. Within it, you will work as a group, with individual directorial responsibility for one **scene** or section of your devised drama. This will involve working from stimuli material to write, direct, design and perform in an original, contemporary theatre performance. There are two outcomes for this unit:

1. Use complex drama skills
2. Contribute creatively to the drama

OUTCOME 1: USE COMPLEX DRAMA SKILLS

1.1 Responding to stimuli, including text, to develop ideas for drama

You will develop your drama from a stimulus. The stimuli could be drawn from a variety of sources: a theatre text, theatre company, poem, newspapers, music, title, theme – the list goes on. Wherever the stimulus material is drawn from, the process is the same. You will work through a range of stimuli, before choosing one to develop into a performance.

1.2 Exploring form, genre, structure and style

Experimentation is key here. You can draw on all your drama experiences and try out different styles, performance techniques and dramatic conventions before deciding on how you will present your drama.

1.3 Developing and communicating ideas

Throughout the process, you will need to keep a record of your progress, present your ideas and research to your teacher/group, and communicate through discussion, presentation and performance.

OUTCOME 2: CONTRIBUTE CREATIVELY TO THE DRAMA

2.1 Planning, devising and directing drama

You will create and direct your own piece of drama. Recording your progress in a logbook or diary is useful, in addition to planning your rehearsals clearly and writing a **script** which can be annotated with your blocking, or creating a 'dramatic commentary' which details your direction and justification.

2.2 Using complex acting skills to portray a character

In addition to directing your own drama, or section of a group piece, you will also act in your peers' devised dramas. It is important that you develop your characterisation along their expectations and direction, but you will also be assessed on your performance as an actor.

2.3 Evaluating own work and that of others

Using the logbooks and notes you have created throughout the unit, you will **evaluate** your success both as an actor and as a director. You will also analyse the work of those you have directed throughout the process.

DON'T FORGET

Don't reject out of hand any stimulus material or idea for being 'silly'. Discuss it with others or come back to it later. You never know – it might trigger something brilliant!

THE PROCESS OF DEVISING DRAMA

The stimulus from which you create your drama could be virtually anything. However, the process of devising from the chosen stimulus is always the same. This process is outlined below and, although you might not undertake it in exactly this order, you should ensure that each point is covered as you create your drama.

- Responding to stimuli by offering ideas
- Using drama techniques/conventions
- Identifying appropriate ideas associated with the stimuli and linked texts
- Improvisation and experimentation with concepts, **scenarios** and situations
- Deciding on genre and style
- Deciding on form and structure
- Research
- Ideas for characters and roles
- Ideas for situation and **setting**
- Selecting and rejecting ideas
- Rehearsal
- Ongoing evaluation
- Characterisation techniques
- Using voice and movement to portray character
- Ideas for design
- Performance
- Evaluation

In the Drama Skills unit, you are assessed individually. However, creating drama is seldom a purely individual process and you will need to work closely with others to develop your ideas and create a quality piece of work. You should take inspiration from theatre companies, movies, books, play texts, current affairs, music, your peers – everything and everyone around you. Throughout the process, you will encounter issues and problems, but through perseverance and teamwork you will succeed.

Working relationships

When devising and rehearsing, it is important that positive working relationships are created. You may not particularly like someone on a personal level, but you have to find a way of working with them in order to succeed. On the following pages, there are some suggestions of activities that can help create positive, collaborative working relationships which can be built upon throughout the process.

 THINGS TO DO AND THINK ABOUT

Make a plan.

Consider the amount of time you have to create and perform your drama. Think about how long you will need to spend on each part of the process and create a timeline for your work. This plan may change throughout the process, but keep the end point in sight and alter your process accordingly.

INFLUENCES ON THEATRE

Consider what you want your drama to say – what **message** you want the audience to leave with. Throughout its history, theatre has developed and changed, reflecting what is occurring in the real world. There are a number of factors that shape theatre, and it strongly reflects the social, political and technical backdrop on which it is created.

SOCIAL INFLUENCE

There are many examples of how society affects the theatre being created and, throughout your textual and performance analysis work (see later chapters), you will become increasingly aware of how theatre reflects and/or challenges the society for which it was written.

An example of this is *The Importance of Being Earnest* written by Oscar Wilde in 1890. The play, tagged as 'a trivial play for serious people', echoes upper-class Victorian societal values and attitudes. It is essentially a **melodrama**, with cases of mistaken identity, double lives and falling in love. However, from the very outset it is apparent that Oscar Wilde is reflecting the society he was writing for, and much of the comedy comes from familiarity. Victorians felt that it was of the utmost importance to be seen to do the right thing, which might involve following a code of manners and politeness while demonstrating little humour (being earnest). Throughout the play, Oscar Wilde clearly highlights the hypocrisy of these rules and how comical they actually were.

Throughout theatrical history as well as in contemporary theatre, there are countless examples of plays that reflect the social situations and views of the **period** and the social group the play was written about.

The Importance of Being Earnest

POPULAR CULTURE

Theatre often reflects popular culture and the tastes of the audience it was written to attract. This can be done by using music and references to TV, film and social media, and reflecting them in performance. These references cement a theatrical performance in its setting, but can also be used to update and revive a play and set it in a new context. Many of Shakespeare's plays, for example, have been reworked or reimagined to make them relevant to a contemporary audience. Theatre director Nicholas Hytner has staged many innovative productions of Shakespearean classics and has often set these productions in a time and place that is different from the original. His production of *Othello* in 2013, for example, used modern fashion and music to remove the 400-year-old setting, which for many today is difficult to understand. By demystifying the context and making it closer to its audience, it becomes easier to understand the meaning of the play and its themes and issues.

ONLINE

Read more about Nicholas Hytner's production of *Othello* at www.brightredbooks.net

POLITICAL INFLUENCE

Politics plays a huge part in theatre. *The Cheviot, the Stag and the Black, Black Oil* by John McGrath was first performed by the 7:84 Theatre Company (so called as, at the time, 7 per cent of the population held 84 per cent of the UK's wealth) in 1974. The play charts the history of the Highland Clearances through to the discovery of oil in the North Sea and how this has affected the communities of the Highlands and north-east of Scotland. The play was very political and had a resonance for many in Scotland and beyond because, at the time, the SNP were using the campaign slogan 'It's Scotland's Oil'. As was apparent in the 2014 independence referendum, the ownership and control of this resource is still politically important today. The play toured rural, non-theatre **venues** throughout Scotland and its theatrical influence can still be seen in contemporary theatre – notably in the National Theatre of Scotland.

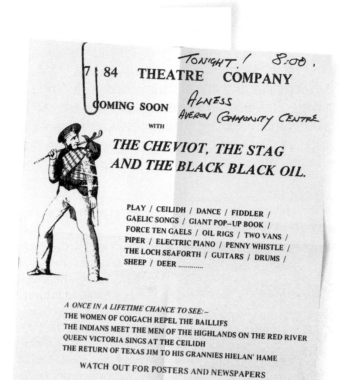

PLAYWRIGHTS' INTENTIONS

Many writers in all genres write from their own experience. Whether writing in their own dialect or focusing on an issue they are passionate about, the voice of **playwrights** is heard through their work. Historically, this is sometimes in a rather veiled manner, and it is only now that we are free to learn about a playwright's background so that we can read more into what influenced his or her writing. For example, in Shakespeare's *Hamlet* we see a play that is preoccupied with corruption and death. Shakespeare himself had been faced with the death of both his son (who was called Hamnet) and his father not long before writing the play. We can now imagine how these experiences might have influenced him in writing it. Of course, he himself was neither royal nor from Denmark! Whether a playwright has a political or social reason for writing a play or is simply writing autobiographically or allegorically, we can discover much about a play by learning about its writer.

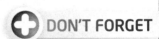 **DON'T FORGET**

Theatre is rarely simplistic and there are always outside influences on the creation of quality drama performances. To really understand a theatrical performance you must understand its context fully.

TECHNOLOGICAL ADVANCES

Advances in technology have had a great influence on how theatre is performed. From the invention of electric lighting to modern digital technology, many discoveries have altered how scenery is created and **action** is presented onstage. Many theatre companies are embracing developments in technology and are developing innovative ways of telling stories.

 ONLINE

For more on technology's influence on theatre, follow the link at www.brightredbooks.net

 THINGS TO DO AND THINK ABOUT

What do you want to create theatre about?

Is there a particular theme, news story, experience or book that could inspire you when creating your drama? Make a list of societal and political issues that affect you and your life. You may be surprised by what could make an interesting piece of drama.

 ONLINE TEST

Test yourself on the influences on theatre at www.brightredbooks.net

CONTEMPORARY THEATRE

Theatre in Scotland and all over the world is currently taking risks, combining styles and genres, utilising mixed media and exploring how theatre can keep up with the digital age. It is quite an exciting time and, although many 'new' performance concepts can be traced back to previous practitioners and playwrights, the combination of current styles and sense of experimentation appeals to audiences, and therefore creates incredibly successful productions.

THE NATIONAL THEATRE OF SCOTLAND

Black Watch

Believe it or not, there was no national theatre company in Scotland until 2006 when the National Theatre of Scotland was formed. The mission was to create a 'theatre without walls' which was not confined to a particular theatre building but would travel throughout the country to bring innovative theatre to the people. The company collaborates with playwrights, established theatres such as The Lyceum in Edinburgh and The Citizens in Glasgow, and also with the general public through its various projects and the Learn programme. One of the company's earliest collaborations was with playwright Gregory Burke and Frantic Assembly's Steven Hoggett during the Edinburgh Festival of 2006. The National Theatre of Scotland carried out its promise to deliver ground-breaking theatre for the people of Scotland and the world in the seminal worldwide phenomenon *Black Watch*. Through collaborations and its choices in creating new work, as well as reviving Scottish classics like *The Guid Sisters* and *Men Should Weep* and reimagining classics like *A Midsummer Night's Dream* and *Peter Pan*, the National Theatre of Scotland has managed to find a niche as a company whose audiences will be open to experiment, in the knowledge that what they see will be good and may surprise them. Not bad for a young company!

THE NATIONAL THEATRE

Traditionally, the National Theatre was a straight-laced and worthy company. However, in recent times it has become reinvigorated, creating original theatre with mass appeal. Recent productions, such as *War Horse, One Man, Two Guvnors* and *The Curious Incident of the Dog in the Night-Time*, have seen the company reinvigorate the old and embrace the new. Through collaboration and **innovation**, the company is currently producing some acclaimed and important work. The National Theatre is able to stage large-scale productions which are often epic and visually stunning while still being able to stage classic texts. The company has an excellent reputation and is almost guaranteed to sell a production on its name alone, making it a powerhouse in the UK theatre landscape.

The Curious Incident of the Dog in the Night-Time – National Theatre, photo by Brinkhoff/Mögenburg

FRANTIC ASSEMBLY

From seemingly humble beginnings, this company has managed to take the alternative and make it mainstream. It was heavily influenced by DV8, a company formed in 1994 which by its own admission did not initially rise to the challenge. Through mixing clear narrative and physical action, Frantic Assembly creates emotive, often amusing and truly inspiring work, which has been recognised and used by both the National Theatre of Scotland and the National Theatre to create interesting and engaging drama.

 DON'T FORGET

Theatre companies provide a huge variety of information and resources online. Utilise their websites in order to research and develop your awareness of the companies' work.

GECKO THEATRE COMPANY

Gecko is a **physical theatre** company which puts its audience at the centre of the action. Its work is actively created to be open to interpretation. It utilises social media in order to interact with and engage with its audience. The process of developing a new Gecko production is long and intensive and includes a 'creative tour' where the company begins to perform the production while still altering and developing it. The company actively works to promote its work to young audiences: 'We have a responsibility to our audiences, especially our young audiences, to produce the most exciting, powerful, challenging work possible – a responsibility we take very seriously.'

 THINGS TO DO AND THINK ABOUT

Choose one of the theatre companies mentioned above. Research this company and consider how it presents the stories it chooses to tell. You may like to investigate:

- The history of the company
- Its aims
- Awards and recognition
- Collaborations
- Notable productions
- Influences
- Audience responses to productions
- Your own interpretation and opinion of the company's work

Keep a record of what you have discovered as this could influence what you create and the style in which you present it. Your teacher will be looking for a clear progression and through-line from your initial research to the final piece.

 ONLINE

Check out the websites of these theatre companies at www.brightredbooks.net

ONLINE TEST

Head to www.brightredbooks.net and test yourself on contemporary theatre.

INITIAL IDEAS

In the early stages, you will need to work fairly collaboratively with others in order to decide on the stimulus, **storyline** or concept and the themes and issues which will be explored through the performance. Much of this will involve discussion and deliberation. However, you must also ensure that you document your work in some sort of folio form so that you can complete an evaluation of your work (both folio and evaluation will be covered later in the chapter). Within this section, we will explore possible ways of approaching the practical aspects of this stage, and look at how you can take on responsibility for your section in addition to contributing to others' work. We will follow the first few points of the **drama process** in order to investigate how you can explore your initial ideas for drama.

TEAM-BUILDING

This unit tends to be taught at the beginning of the course or concurrently (at the same time) with the Production Skills unit. You may well be working with people you aren't used to, or those you know quite well and have worked with before. Either way, it is important that you ensure you build positive working relationships so that you can create a polished performance at the end of the unit. Below are some examples of tasks you could undertake in order to build positive, creative working relationships before you have even begun to look at stimulus materials.

'Getting to know you' games

 ACTIVITY: TWO TRUTHS/ONE LIE

In pairs, each person tells the other two facts about himself or herself and one whopping great lie. The other person then presents these back to the rest of the group as their own information. The trick for the remainder of the group is to spot the lie.

ACTIVITY: ABOUT ME

Each person writes an unknown fact about themself on a sticky note or piece of paper. These are then drawn from a hat (or bag) and the group tries to guess who the fact is about.

ACTIVITY: KNOTS

The group stands in a circle and each person takes the hands of two different people across the circle. The task is then to 'untie' the knot without breaking contact.

After you have begun to gel as a group, you could undertake some improvisation-style games which will further build trust and help your group to find out more about its strengths and weaknesses in terms of acting and performance. You will probably have tried a number of improvisation exercises previously and can draw from your own experiences here. Here are a couple of examples of improvisation games to get you started.

ACTIVITY: PARK BENCH

A character is minding their own business sitting on a park bench. A second character enters the scene with the objective of making the first character feel so awkward they wish to leave. The remainder of the group can shout 'Freeze!' at any point and take the place of either character to change the scene.

contd

ONLINE

There are a number of good websites with a variety of drama games and exercises available. Try the Drama Toolkit at www.brightredbooks.net for starters – it breaks down games and activities into types so it is easy to find what you are looking for.

ACTIVITY: GIVEN CIRCUMSTANCES

Pairs or groups are provided with **'given circumstances'** – a time, place and action or objective. The group then improvises a short scene using the information given. For example, Time: The morning war was declared; Place: On a mountainside; Action: A precious item has gone missing.

RESPONDING TO STIMULUS BY OFFERING IDEAS

Now that you have begun to bond as a group, you can begin to look at how to approach the task of developing ideas from a stimulus. There are a number of ways of doing this: mind-mapping, discussion, improvisation and practical exploration. People have different preferences and it is important that you bear this in mind as you come up with your initial ideas, giving everyone in your group the time and freedom they need to contribute constructively. The following is an example of how you could go about developing initial ideas from a choice of stimuli.

Mind-mapping

Mind-mapping is an important part of communicating your thoughts: to your group, your teacher and your future self. An initial mind-map can be returned to later, to reinvigorate an idea or revisit your reasons for choosing it. A mind-map could be described as 'your brain on a page' and you should be encouraged to use colour, pictures and highlighting, or whatever else you wish, to demonstrate your thoughts on a particular stimulus. Mind-maps are personal, but can also be very useful in communicating your ideas to others.

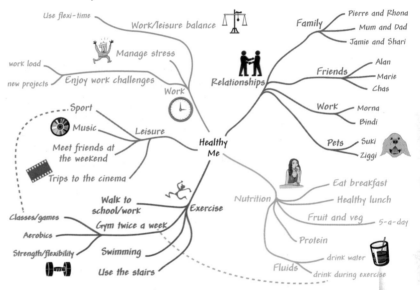

 ACTIVITY: STIMULI TASKS

1 Watch the trailer at http://www.digitaltheatre.com/production and read the blurb for a play of your choice on digital theatre. Make a list of what you think are the central themes of the play. From this list of themes mind-map your ideas for a drama.

2 The quotation below comes from the novel *The Curious Incident of the Dog in the Night-Time* by Mark Haddon. Underline interesting words, phrases and concepts within the text. Consider what pictures it conjures and how these could be used as the basis of a drama. You could focus on a single word or concept, or the extract as a whole.

> And when the universe has finished exploding all the stars will slow down, like a ball has been thrown into the air, and they will come to a halt and they will all begin to fall towards the centre of the universe again. And then there will be nothing to stop us seeing all the stars in the world because they will all be moving towards us, gradually faster and faster, and we will know that the world is going to end soon because when we look into the sky at night there will be no darkness, just the blazing light of billions and billions of stars, all falling.

 DON'T FORGET

No idea is a bad idea at this stage. Something that you initially think is useless or silly could spark another idea when you revisit it, or it could link to an idea that someone else in the group has had!

 THINGS TO DO AND THINK ABOUT

Once you have completed the two tasks above, share your ideas with others and talk them through. Through discussion and negotiation you should come up with a **focus** for the drama you wish to create.

 ONLINE TEST

Test yourself on this topic online at www.brightredbooks.net

REFINED IDEAS — DEVELOPMENT

Through your work in the previous pages, you should have a variety of ideas that you could pursue. Within this section, we will explore how you can hone these ideas and begin to form a more focused concept. It is important to note that, even once you have settled on an idea or concept, there is still much room for development and it can take a bit of time to reach a polished performance.

RESEARCH AND EXPERIMENTATION

Once you have ideas to develop, it is important that you research them. It is relatively easy to conduct initial research online or through discussing the idea with your group, your peers, teacher and family. Through this research you may discover interesting true-life stories, films, books, paintings, music or plays which relate to your chosen idea. You should be able to develop and refine your concept further and shape it into something which can be communicated theatrically. At this stage, it should become apparent whether your group will be taking on responsibility for telling a part of a larger story, or if you will be telling individual stories which are linked by a central theme.

Example:

Let's think about a drama based around the theme of 'appearance versus reality'.

Student 1 is responsible for scene 1, where the central protagonist is faced with a tragedy and finds it difficult to deal with it. The scene ends with her alone onstage speaking to herself in the mirror, blaming herself for her friend's death.

Student 2 takes on responsibility for scene 2, where the protagonist begins to interact with another version of herself which she sees in the mirror. Her friend visits and she manages to keep up appearances while often being distracted by her vision in the mirror.

Student 3 is responsible for the third scene. In this scene there is a physical theatre section where the protagonist battles with two other versions of herself. Her friend then arrives and, realising there is something wrong, comforts her and calls for help.

The final scene is a group effort. Using a pre-filmed projection of what the protagonist is experiencing in her head – the different versions of herself and voices of people in her life – she discusses her problems with a psychiatrist. Throughout the scene she becomes more positive and the voices and confusion in her head (on screen) become more clear.

contd

The second approach, where each person tells their own story related to the same theme, could be structured in a variety of ways – a particular event from different characters' perspectives, for example, or completely unrelated scenes which explore the same theme. Whichever approach you take, it is vitally important that you make a rehearsal schedule to ensure that each group member has an equal opportunity to develop their scene/section.

Once you have researched, discussed and decided on the broad structure of the drama, you can begin to experiment with **plot**, structure, conventions, scenarios, characters and situations. Again, there are a variety of ways of doing this, but there are two broad styles which most individuals prefer to use. The first is through improvisation; the second through detailed scripting. At some point in the process the two approaches usually merge, but how that actually happens is quite a personal thing.

Other approaches

- **Scenario/given circumstances** – The actors are provided with detailed information about their character and the scene they are to improvise. As the actors perform their scene, they either film it or make an audio recording of what they have come up with. You can then work from the recording when writing your script.

- **Script writing** – If you are basing your drama on a real-life event or another text, you may wish to develop your script with close reference to the text. You can then take the script to the next rehearsal and work through it with your actors. You may wish to edit as you go, or make detailed notes on your script to be rewritten or developed in your own time.

Whichever approach you take, it will result in several draft copies of the script as you develop it. You should aim to produce a final script or detailed scenario to work from in the final performance, as you will undoubtedly wish to have accurate **cues** etc. written down. Your teacher will probably wish to see a copy of the script in good time before the performance, in order to support you in the development of your scene or section.

ONLINE

For some advice from successful playwright Zinnie Harris, head to www.brightredbooks.net

DON'T FORGET

As you develop your script, you should involve your actors as much as possible to ensure both they and you fully understand the text and how it links to other group members' sections.

How many playwrights does it take to change a light bulb?

I'm not changing anything!

THINGS TO DO AND THINK ABOUT

At the end of the unit you, will be required to evaluate your performance throughout the process. It is essential that you keep a detailed log of rehearsals and how you have developed your scene or section.

ONLINE TEST

To test yourself on the development of ideas, head to www.brightredbooks.net

FINAL IDEAS

The most obvious communication of your final concepts and ideas will be through the performance. In order to ensure everything is communicated through the performance, you will have to have had ample opportunity to rehearse and refine your concepts with your actors, in addition to planning and plotting any technical performance cues. Finally, you will also need to ensure you perform to the best of your ability as an actor in at least one scene or section (depending on group size you will probably appear in several). The formation of your final ideas and concepts begins from the first read-through of your script. Between then and the final performance, there is a lot that can happen and you will change and adapt your ideas throughout.

FINAL IDEAS WITHIN EACH ROLE

Within the rehearsal process for the Drama Skills unit, you have two clear roles: director/ deviser and actor. The responsibilities and processes for these roles are different. You must be organised; planning is the key to success in this process. The following practices could assist you in reaching and documenting your final ideas successfully.

Director/deviser

Before each rehearsal, make a clear plan and share this with your cast. You should detail the overall aim for the rehearsal and the aspects to be addressed, in addition to offering notes throughout the rehearsal. At the end of the rehearsal you should de-brief your actors and evaluate both your and their performance, in readiness for the next rehearsal.

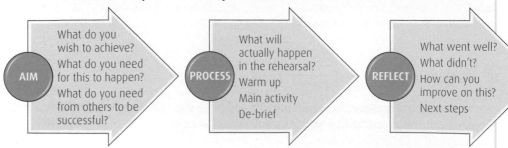

AIM — What do you wish to achieve? What do you need for this to happen? What do you need from others to be successful?

PROCESS — What will actually happen in the rehearsal? Warm up. Main activity. De-brief

REFLECT — What went well? What didn't? How can you improve on this? Next steps

contd

As you come to the end of the rehearsal process and your actors have learned their **lines** and cues, it is important that you do not allow the performance to become stale. To prevent this from happening you must keep your cast 'on their toes'. You may wish to use some of the following rehearsal techniques:

- **Improvisation** – Putting the characters in different contexts and situations can assist your actors in deepening their understanding of the character and add a fresh perspective to the situation. If, for example, you have a scene involving a confrontation, you may wish to get your actors to improvise a scene which builds **tension** through both characters purposely trying to rile each other; the tension built up between the characters should spill over into the scene to be performed onstage.

- **Speed runs** – Running a scene, or the whole piece, at speed can add energy and urgency to it, which you may wish to retain at points in the final performance. Instructing your actors to run rather than walk and to speak as quickly as possible should put pressure on them in terms of knowing lines and cues.

- **Swapping characters** – Through swapping the roles of your actors you may discover new aspects of the character, and this can be very entertaining and energising for both you and the actors.

- **Character development** – In order to ensure you get the best possible performance from your actors, you can help them by assisting in character development. You should discuss with each actor how you see their character and gain an awareness of their viewpoint. Together, you should make new discoveries about the character which will inform both your and the actor's development. You may wish to set tasks such as '**writing** in role' and '**hot seating**' to assist you in doing this.

- **Design** – There will be specific requirements of your script: the **location**, use of props, character appearance and sound and lighting. In order for your drama to be successful, you must ensure you consider aspects of design/production throughout the rehearsal period and begin to implement your **production concepts** as early as possible in the process.

Actor

As an actor, you must ensure you note down all your blocking, are on time and fully briefed for rehearsals, and learn all your lines in good time. You must develop your character fully throughout the rehearsal period.

DISCOURSE

Throughout the entire process of devising, rehearsing and performing a drama, you should be consistently aware of its discourse – all of the aspects of the performance which communicate with the audience. This can be done both literally and metaphorically. The **language** of the characters provides the audience with a great deal of information and you should develop your **dialogue** carefully. However, it is not only spoken language which is a tool in communicating meaning. You also communicate by means of your use of images, through **tableaux**, set pieces, abstract movement, literal movement and projections. Your use of set, props, lighting and costume also communicates a great deal. The overall discourse of the piece should be conceived with a clear **target audience** in mind, and you must carefully consider your choices to ensure your devised performance connects with the audience in attendance.

DON'T FORGET

You must be level-headed in rehearsals and not become too 'precious' over your material. Once you have engaged your actors in bringing the text to life, it belongs as much to them as it does to you, and they may have valuable insights.

ONLINE

Have a look at how the theatre company Frantic Assembly goes about creating theatre in the devising master-class at www.brightredbooks.net

ONLINE TEST

To test yourself on final ideas, head to www.brightredbooks.net

THINGS TO DO AND THINK ABOUT

Consider the different ways you have encountered of creating mood, atmosphere and tension. How can you employ these in your own production?

FOLIO AND EVALUATION

In order to monitor and evidence your work throughout the Drama Skills unit, it is essential that you maintain a folio. A large part of the folio should be your logbook or diary. In addition to this, you should also create notes and information on your process. This supporting portfolio will be assessed alongside your practical performance and evaluation, and it is a vital part of the Drama Skills unit.

SUGGESTED FORMS OF EVIDENCE

The following are suggested forms of evidence which relate directly to the outcomes of the unit.

1.1 Responding to stimuli, including text to develop ideas for drama

Your responses and notes relating to the stimuli tasks. These may be mind-maps, scenarios, details of the possible message and **purpose** of the drama, evaluative comments on your own and others' progress.

1.2 Exploring form, genre, structure and style

Details of your research into the possible time and setting of the drama; you can display this in a variety of ways – posters, mind-maps, PowerPoint presentations, collages, mood boards etc. You can also provide overviews of your improvisation plans by outlining your chosen given circumstances and how you lead initial rehearsals. Any rehearsal plans should also be included, in addition to a clear rehearsal schedule, a detailed scenario and/or script, and character overviews for your actors.

1.3 Developing and communicating ideas

A detailed description of performance concept, annotated script, rehearsal notes and plans, ongoing evaluation, filmed or photographed rehearsals.

2.1 Planning, devising and directing drama

Annotated script, rehearsal schedule, notes for actors and next steps, filmed or photographed rehearsals.

2.2 Using complex acting skills to portray character to an audience

Continued evaluation through logbook/diary, character notes, filmed and photographed rehearsals, final performance.

2.3 Evaluating own and others' performance

Ongoing evaluation through the logbook/diary and summative evaluation after the performance.

LOGBOOK

You should keep a log of your progress throughout the entire process. This will help you to reflect on and assess your work, in addition to being a revision tool when it comes to completing the evaluation task at the end of the unit. When completing your logbook, you should look back on the planning notes you have made for the rehearsal and use these as a basis for your ongoing evaluative work in the logbook. Here is an example logbook entry.

contd

Example:

Rehearsal Date: Mon. 12 Sept.

Focus/aim of rehearsal – The main aim for this rehearsal is to develop the second scene, where Pete discovers his son is missing. This scene needs to be filled with tension, and through exercises and improvisation I will establish ways of creating the necessary level of tension for the scene to be successful.

Process – I will initially play the game 'Mafia' with the cast, as this game raises suspicion among its participants and can be very tense. I will then explain the given circumstances of the scene and get the cast to improvise the scene. I will also experiment with this further, giving the different characters different levels of tension to play. I will record the improvisations throughout in order to help me with my scripting of the scene.

Successes – The rehearsal was incredibly successful in developing dialogue for my scene. The cast cooperated with me and with each other extremely well and created tension which should translate to the final scene, once I have tweaked the dialogue.

Areas for improvement – Generally it was a good rehearsal. However, I think the cast could improve their focus, as at points when I was trying to address the serious central issue they were giggling and making light of it.

Target for next rehearsal – I will try to use a focusing exercise at the beginning of the rehearsal in an attempt to keep my cast concentrating throughout. I will also write up a script for the scene for further development.

EVALUATION

Following your performance, you will be required to complete an evaluation of your work throughout the process and in the final performance. Within this evaluation you will also evaluate the work of your cast and your performance as an actor. There are different approaches to the evaluation: you may be given a series of questions or be asked to write an essay. It may be prepared as homework, but is written up under supervision and controlled conditions. It is an essential part of the unit assessment and without an evaluation you would not pass the unit. The following is an example of an evaluation carried out using the essay method. The evaluation, like the practical assessment, is assessed on a pass/fail basis.

Example:

Introduction
Overview of the performance your group created. Where and when it took place, the target audience, the audience in attendance, the venue, the style and subject matter of the piece.
This should be brief.

Part 1: Rehearsal
Describe how you developed your section from stimulus to performance. You should refer to both your own performance as a director and designer and also to the performance of your cast of actors during the devising and rehearsal period.

1. Stimulus: explain how you settled on a stimulus, why you chose it and how you began to develop it.

2. Describe the themes and issues of your drama.

3. Director: describe your performance as a director during the rehearsal process.

4. Actor: describe your performance as an actor during rehearsal.

Part 2: Performance
1. Describe and evaluate the impact of your section on the assembled audience. You should comment on your actors' performances, the impact of your design and the effectiveness of your direction.

2. Describe your performance as an actor. You should comment on your use of voice, movement, and characterisation to create the desired impact on the audience.

Conclusion
Overall, what were the successes/weaknesses of your performance over the unit? How do you know what they were and how will you improve your work?

DON'T FORGET

You can discuss your acting in other people's sections.

ONLINE

You can see a more detailed plan and an example folio at www.brightredbooks.net

ONLINE TEST

To test yourself on the folio and evaluation, head to www.brightredbooks.net

 THINGS TO DO AND THINK ABOUT

Ask the audience!

To help you gauge your audience's response to your direction and acting, ask them to complete a quick appraisal of your performance. This will help you complete the evaluation successfully.

PRODUCTION SKILLS

THE PRODUCTION PROCESS

In this chapter, we will explore the requirements of the Production Skills unit of Higher Drama. We will look at possible ways of approaching and structuring your work throughout the unit, in addition to exploring methods of approaching and analysing text and developing production concepts.

This unit will develop your ability to design and perform a production. Within it, you will work as a group, with individual responsibility for two or more production skills. There are two outcomes for this unit:

1. The candidate will analyse a range of production skills.
2. The candidate will apply a range of production skills.

OUTCOME 1: THE CANDIDATE WILL ANALYSE A RANGE OF PRODUCTION SKILLS

1.1 Responding to stimuli, including text, to generate ideas for production

You will develop a drama from a stimulus, which could come from a variety of sources, but is often (though not always) the text you will study for the textual analysis essay.

1.2 Applying a range of production skills to communicate ideas

You will develop your use of different production roles and apply these skills to the drama performed.

1.3 Evaluating the use of a range of production skills

In addition to completing an evaluation of the whole process at the end of the unit, you should evaluate your progress on an ongoing basis, by means of a diary or logbook.

OUTCOME 2: THE CANDIDATE WILL APPLY A RANGE OF PRODUCTION SKILLS

2.1 Selecting appropriate ideas to develop a performance concept

Through research and experimentation, you will develop a detailed performance concept which demonstrates your understanding of the production process.

2.2 Applying a range of production skills within a production

In preparation for the performance and the performance itself, you will apply your production skills.

2.3 Evaluate their contribution to the drama and that of others

You will analyse how the production team has worked together to reach a shared goal.

APPROACHES TO LEARNING

There are two broad approaches to learning in this unit. The first approach is similar to the drama process where you develop a drama from a stimulus before applying your production skills. The second approach is to develop a production for a text: this may be the text you are studying in preparation for the written exam or another chosen text. You would then apply your skills to an extract from this text in performance. Whichever approach you take, this chapter will cover the production process from the point at which the plot of a devised drama is established or the text is chosen. For the remainder of this section, the word 'text' should be understood to cover both a devised script and a published play text. The outline below describes the production process and, although you might not undertake it in the exact order here, you should ensure that each point is covered as you develop the performance.

- Analysing the text

- Researching the context and setting

- Choosing your role (acting, directing or design) bearing in mind that you must experience two or more roles

- Researching the role with reference to the requirements of the text

- Presenting initial concepts to others

- Discussing and developing concepts

- Taking part in production meetings

- Developing a final production concept

- Applying production concepts to a performance

Preparing a text for performance is a collaborative activity. However, you are assessed individually for the Production Skills unit. You must negotiate with others at an early stage to agree on a broad concept, and on an ongoing basis to develop your concepts individually. The establishment of positive working relationships is just as important in this unit as it is in the Drama Skills unit (see previous chapter for guidance on this). However, you must also have self-discipline, as you may well spend a proportion of your time working alone to develop ideas before applying them in rehearsal and performance.

 ## THINGS TO DO AND THINK ABOUT

Plan ahead.

It is important that you create some form of plan or schedule for the development of your production. This timeline may alter as you progress through the process but should be established at an early stage. Within your plan or schedule, ensure that you include time for production meetings. This is time set aside for the whole team to come together and discuss the development of their relevant areas, to ensure that they are coherent and complementary. You should keep a clear record of these meetings, which might be in the form of agendas and minutes. Creating an agenda beforehand will help bring a clear focus to discussions, and taking down detailed minutes or making an audio recording of the meeting will help remind each group member of what was discussed and any associated tasks that they may need to carry out before the next meeting.

 ONLINE

For more information on how performance concepts are realised in the three areas of acting, directing and design, there are a number of videos you can view at www.brightredbooks.net

 DON'T FORGET

Developing a production concept is an individual task, but you must liaise closely with the other members of your team to ensure it is coherent.

 ONLINE TEST

Test yourself on the production process at www.brightredbooks.net

PRODUCTION SKILLS

ANALYSING A TEXT

Whether you are working from a devised script or published text, you should analyse the text in a similar way. This is an important part of the production skills process, as it informs your interpretation and will be instrumental in developing your concepts for the performance of the piece.

ONLINE

You can find notes for a number of published plays either online or from bookshops. Education Scotland provides free resources for the following texts which are on the recommended text list: *The Importance of Being Earnest, Twelfth Night, The Birthday Party, The House of Bernarda Alba, A Taste of Honey, Ghosts, Lovers, Mother Courage and Her Children, The Crucible, Waiting for Godot, The Merchant of Venice, Antigone*. Follow the link at www.brightredbooks.net for more information.

APPROACHING ANALYSIS

Approaching analysis can seem like a rather daunting process. However, like most things, when it is broken down into smaller activities or steps it is much easier to approach. The following is a suggestion of how you might approach your analysis, although this might vary depending on the play you are planning to perform.

Read the text

This seems quite obvious. However, there is much more to this than simply reading through the text in its entirety, although this is a good way to start! The first reading should be just that: try to read the play in one sitting so that you get an overall feel for the piece and how it might come over in performance. Following this, you may wish to get together with others and read it aloud. At this point you can begin to develop a sense of the characters' personalities and attitudes. The reading doesn't end here, as you should then read the play, or at least specific parts of the text, from the perspective of an actor, director or designer, noting down requirements as you go.

Research the setting and context

In order to get a good background knowledge of the play, you should conduct research into it. You can use study guides, online resources, books, TV documentaries, radio interviews or any other appropriate media to do this. The main areas you should research are:

- the time and place setting of the play
- the playwright's life and other work
- the political/social/religious/theatrical context of the text
- the popular culture of the **time period** (art, music, literature, TV, cinema, etc.)
- the themes and issues associated with the text
- the characters and relationships
- the first performance
- other notable productions.

DON'T FORGET

Remember to keep a bibliography as you go of any websites or books you use as your research.

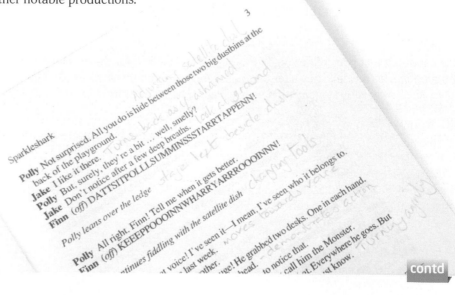

contd

Your research should be fairly extensive and documented to help you develop your concepts for the performance.

Analysis of themes

Following your research into the play, you should be able to draw out particular themes and issues from the text. Consider how these themes are being explored and highlight specific examples.

Character representations

You should consider what each character represents and how the character develops throughout the text. You could ask yourself some questions to help you do this:

- Are there particular actions or relationships within the text that highlight themes or issues?
- Is the character representative of a particular attitude or belief?
- How do the characters react and relate to each other, and what does this communicate?
- Is the character a representation of a particular type?
- What is the purpose of the character in the text?

Mood, atmosphere and tension

Consider the **mood** and **atmosphere** of the play and how it alters throughout. How do you know what the atmosphere is? How has the writer created it? You may like to note down any changes in mood and atmosphere, and how they are triggered: for example, is it when a character enters or leaves the scene or when a particular piece of information is provided? Think about how you could highlight this change in performance.

Symbols and metaphors

Are there any aspects of the text which represent something else? For example, a candle burning out onstage represents the extinguishing of a life offstage. You should look at how the writer has created these metaphors and consider how you could highlight this in performance.

Once you have built up a good bank of notes providing detailed analysis of the text, you will be ready to start exploring the text from the three different perspectives of acting, directing and design.

DON'T FORGET

Keep a written record of all your analysis, as it sets you up well for your practical exploration into the text.

 THINGS TO DO AND THINK ABOUT

Question your sources.

A great deal of what is written about a text is opinion. While you research and analyse the text, you should be building your own opinion and interpretation about what certain aspects represent and mean. If you discover a 'fact' about the text, make sure you can corroborate it. As a rule, three sources that agree on the 'fact' probably make it true! As you go through the analysis process, discuss your findings with your teacher and peers, and make copious notes that you will be able to reflect on and use later.

 ONLINE TEST

Head to www.brightredbooks.net and test yourself on analysing a text.

DEVELOPING PERFORMANCE CONCEPTS

In the following section, we will explore the process of developing your performance concepts and presenting these in the final performance. You should also refer to the next chapter, which focuses on each specialism, its responsibilities and associated tasks in much more detail.

APPROACHES TO LEARNING

It is a requirement of the unit that you apply a range of production skills (a range is defined as two or more). It is advisable that you gain experience of each specialism – acting, directing and design – but if this is not possible it is probably a good idea to undertake the two roles you have least experience of, as this will help you in other areas of the course and assist your choices for the final exam. It may be that you can structure your work in such a way that you can split your text into two or three sections and take on a different role in each. Or, you may decide to undertake two roles simultaneously. Whichever approach you take, it is useful to structure the development of your concepts into three broad sections:

- initial ideas and concepts
- developed concepts
- final concepts.

You should also ensure that you have time to meet as a whole production team, to communicate with other members of your group and make certain you are all working towards a shared goal.

Initial ideas and concepts

Whichever specialism(s) you are working on, there are similarities in terms of the tasks and activities you should be undertaking at each point in the process. Your initial ideas and concepts should encompass all the analytical and research work you have undertaken, and show some consideration for the requirements of the area you are focusing on. For all roles, you should have some broad ideas and be able to present these ideas to your class, group or teacher. You can present your ideas in a variety of ways and should be encouraged to use a variety of means:

- a verbal presentation
- a PowerPoint presentation
- a mood board
- mind-maps
- handouts
- photographs
- video clips
- or any other relevant means.

Following this initial presentation, and subsequent discussion, you should be able to undertake further research, experiment with ways of creating a given concept and deepen your understanding of the role.

contd

Developed concepts

During this stage of the process, the activities you will be involved in will differ depending on which area you are specialising in. If you are working on two areas simultaneously, you must ensure you are giving both of them an appropriate amount of focus to make the performance effective overall.

Actor – As an actor, you should be focusing your attention on developing your character, undertaking detailed characterisation work and marking all of your blocking down during rehearsals. You could also be involved with costume and props decisions, as you should be forming a clear idea of your character's personality and you will have an understanding of, or at least an opinion on, how the character would dress and the possessions they may have.

Director – As a director, you must focus on making blocking decisions and communicating with your actors and designer. You should plan your rehearsals carefully and have a clear aim for each one, which should be communicated to your team at the start. You should also be beginning to create a prompt copy, with details of all blocking decisions and cues.

Designer – As a designer, you should be experimenting and sourcing during this period. You should be in frequent contact with the other members of your group to ensure your design choices are remaining relevant to the shared vision of the piece and are not going to hinder the performance in any way.

Final concepts

In essence, your final concepts, whichever area you are working on, are the performance itself. However, there are also supplementary tasks which should be carried out to ensure the concepts are realised in the performance.

Actor – Final decisions on the use of voice, movement and characterisation should be made and maintained in rehearsal and performance. You should also be able to provide a written description of how you will portray the character.

Director – You must oversee any technical or dress rehearsals and have a final, completed prompt copy of your script which can be cross-referenced with what appears onstage. This will help you to evaluate later on. You must also provide a final ground plan.

Designer – You should be able to provide plans, sketches, mood boards, and cue sheets of your set, lighting, costume, props, sound, make-up and hair. You may also be responsible for running parts of the tech/dress rehearsals. During the performance, you will need to check that your designs are ready and in good order.

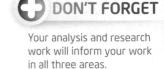
DON'T FORGET

Your analysis and research work will inform your work in all three areas.

ONLINE

Head to www.brightredbooks.net to see an example folio.

 THINGS TO DO AND THINK ABOUT

Take your time!

It is very tempting to try to get the text up on its feet and performed as soon as possible. However, if you rush what might be seen as the boring parts of the process – researching, reading, analysing and discussing the text and your plans for it – you risk not having enough resources to draw from in the later stages. It is also important to recognise that individuals work in different ways and at different **paces**, and it is important to respect others' needs as you progress through the production process.

 ONLINE TEST

To test yourself on developing performance concepts, head to www.brightredbooks.net

FOLIO AND EVALUATION

You should maintain a detailed folio for each specialism – acting, directing and design – to document your work throughout the process, including evaluation and reflection. The folio should include detailed notes relating to the initial, developed and final concepts outlined previously. In addition to this, detailed logbooks and rehearsal plans should be kept to ensure there is a very accurate account of your process in all three specialisms.

LOGBOOKS

The content of your rehearsal logbooks for Production Skills should be targeted, detailed and evaluative. It should reflect each part of the process and form a good account of your development. You could use the questions below in addition to the standard, 'what went well, what didn't, and next steps' used in the Drama Skills unit to help you make detailed observations and evaluative comments regarding your performance in each role.

- What did you do for research and what did you discover that has informed your initial concepts?
- After sharing your initial ideas with the production team, how will you alter and refine your initial concepts?
- How well have you and your group worked as a production team (thus far)? You should detail what each member has contributed to the process as well as the strengths, and points for improvement, of your group members and yourself.

Acting

- How have you developed your character using characterisation techniques?
- What new information have you discovered about the character?
- How will this information affect your **portrayal**?
- How have you collaborated/negotiated with your director?
- How have you collaborated/negotiated with your designer?
- What is the impact of these collaborations?
- How have you developed the voice and movement of the character?
- What is the impact of this development?

Directing

- How have your blocking ideas and **staging** concepts altered/developed after discussing them with your cast and designer?
- What new information have you discovered about the text?
- How will you use this information?
- How have you collaborated/negotiated with your actors?
- How have you collaborated/negotiated with your designer?
- What is the impact of these collaborations?
- What developments have you made in terms of the acting style and overall concepts of the production?
- What is the impact of these developments?

Designing

- How have your **design concepts** altered/developed after discussing them with your cast and director?
- How have you collaborated/negotiated with your actors?
- How have you collaborated/negotiated with your director?
- What is the impact of these collaborations?
- What developments have you made in terms of the design and style of the production?
- What is the impact of these developments?

SUPPLEMENTARY EVIDENCE

In addition to your logbooks, each specialist area requires specific evidence to illustrate that you have fulfilled the outcomes of the unit. If you follow the process outlined previously, this evidence should be generated as a by-product of your work throughout the unit. If you are anxious that you may not have gathered enough evidence for a specific role, use the example checklists below. These include possible forms of evidence cross-referenced with the learning outcomes for the unit. You do not need to have all of the items in your folio; there is an element of choice according to what suits your method of working. Examples are possibilities rather than an exhaustive list.

Example:

Acting

1.1 Mind-maps, presentations, acting concepts, initial character decisions.
1.2 Character development: character profiles, iceberg, role on the wall, notes on voice and movement, blocking marked on script, rehearsal logbooks and any other appropriate notes.
1.3 Rehearsal logbooks and evaluation.
2.1 Final character profile, description of voice and movement, logbooks and any other appropriate notes.
2.2 Description of final performance concept, filmed performance, logbooks and other appropriate notes.
2.3 Logbooks and evaluation.

Example:

Directing

1.1 Mind-maps, presentations, acting concepts, initial character decisions.
1.2 Rehearsal plans, blocking notes, diagrams, filmed rehearsals, annotations.
1.3 Rehearsal logbooks and evaluation.
2.1 Prompt copy, final performance concept, rehearsal plans and logbooks.
2.2 Description of final performance concept, filmed performance, logbooks and other appropriate notes.
2.3 Logbooks and evaluation.

Example:

Designing

1.1 Mind-maps, presentations, design concepts, initial design decisions.
1.2 Developed ideas, annotated designs, rehearsal logbooks and any other appropriate notes.
1.3 Rehearsal logbooks and evaluation.
2.1 Final performance concepts, cue sheets, appropriate associated production tasks.
2.2 Description of final performance concept, filmed performance, photographed designs, cue sheets, logbooks and other appropriate notes.
2.3 Logbooks and evaluation.

EVALUATION

As with the drama skills evaluation, there are two approaches to the evaluation task: it can be either an essay or question/answer structure. The following is an example of the latter approach.

Example:

Part 1: Evaluate your own performance

1. Explain your choice of specialism: acting, directing or design.
   What were the main requirements of the role?
   What skills and abilities did you bring to the role?
2. What challenges did you face in this role and how did you tackle them?
3. What was successful about your performance in this role?
4. How could you improve your work further?
Performance Concept
5. What did you hope to communicate?
6. How did you go about achieving the concept?
7. Was it successful?
8. How do you know?
9. How could you improve your work in the future?

Part 2: Evaluate the performance of others

1. Explain the choice of specialism.
   What were the main requirements of the role?
   What skills and abilities did they bring to the role?
2. What challenges did they face in this role and how did they tackle them?
3. What was successful about their performance in this role?
4. How could they improve their work further?

THINGS TO DO AND THINK ABOUT

It is important to share and discuss your ideas with others throughout the process. Devise a clear plan for individual research and development and check in with your counterparts often. It is important that the lines of communication are open at all times.

DON'T FORGET

Your records and logbooks must be detailed because they form the basis of your evaluation.

 ONLINE

Head to www.brightredbooks.net to see an example evaluation.

 ONLINE TEST

Test yourself on the folio and evaluation at www.brightredbooks.net

PRODUCTION ROLES

ROLES AND RESPONSIBILITIES

A theatre production team works best when it works together towards a shared aim. Within the team, there are clear roles and responsibilities for each area of the production. There are eight areas of production: acting, directing, lighting, sound, set design, props, costume, and make-up and hair. Each one has specific requirements and tasks which must be carried out if the team and the performance are to be successful.

In the professional theatre, there are a number of individuals who work together in particular roles to make up the production team. There are design and technical roles in addition to administrative and educational ones.

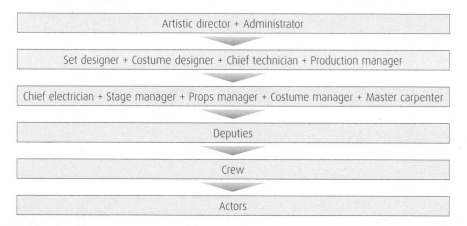

Within the Production Skills unit, you will experiment with different production roles. This will give you a good grounding to decide which role you wish to undertake for the practical assessment towards the end of the course. Here is an overview of the production roles and their associated responsibilities. Each role is then explored in more detail on the following pages.

DON'T FORGET

In order for a production to be successful, all the individuals in the production team must communicate and collaborate to achieve its aim.

ACTING

Without actors, theatre would achieve very little. The actor is a vehicle to communicate the playwright's ideas and director's vision to the audience. Acting is by no means an easy job, there is a great deal of pressure on an actor to achieve the desired performance concepts in front of an audience that has paid to see their work. Their performance can make or break a production and they must be able to cope with criticism and scrutiny from their director and their audience.

Responsibilities

- Read the script closely and make notes on the character.
- Research the setting and the character they are to play.
- Learn lines, and mark moves and instructions from the director on their script.
- Think carefully about appropriate voice and movement for the character.
- Perform their role as the director intended.

DIRECTING

Directing is a fairly new concept in the long history of theatre and only began to evolve in the late nineteenth and early twentieth century. Before this, writers, actors and theatre managers often took on some of the responsibilities usually associated with directors. In the modern theatre, the director is in charge of what happens onstage and works closely with the stage manager, producer, cast and crew to achieve his or her theatrical vision.

contd

Responsibilities

- Have overall control of the production.
- Organise and interpret the text.
- Initiate, coordinate and develop the entire team.
- Oversee the design of the set, lighting, costume, sound, etc.
- Be involved with the actors at all stages from casting, to blocking and performance.
- Have overall control of the budget and its distribution.

LIGHTING

Without lighting, the audience would not be able to see the action onstage. The role of lighting is both technical and design-orientated. You must be able to design an imaginative lighting plot which complements the scenic design, theatrical style, mood and atmosphere, location, costume and characters of the piece, in addition to having the technical skill and health and safety knowledge to achieve the lighting effects.

Responsibilities

- Have knowledge of the equipment and how it can be used.
- Be aware of health and safety issues.
- Liaise with the director, stage manager and costume, props and set designer to reach an agreed design concept for the production and have knowledge of areas/actors to be highlighted, etc.
- Create a lighting plot which is agreed with the director.
- Ensure a rigging plan and lighting plot are made available for the lighting operator.

SOUND

As with lighting, a sound designer/technician must have good technical knowledge. They must also be able to respond creatively to a text and choose or devise sound effects and music which support the creation of mood, atmosphere and tension. In modern theatre, the role of sound is becoming more and more important as technology advances and audience expectations develop.

Responsibilities

- Have knowledge of the equipment and how it can be used.
- Be aware of health and safety issues.
- Liaise with the director, stage manager and costume, props and set designer to reach an agreed design concept for the production.
- Create a sound plot in conjunction with the director.
- Source effects and music requested by the director.
- Create a sound plot that is easy to follow for the operator.

VIDEO LINK

Have a look at how theatre professionals describe their roles at www.brightredbooks.net

THINGS TO DO AND THINK ABOUT

Utilise your outside knowledge and experience.

When choosing which role to pursue, you should consider your talents and outside learning and interests. For example, if you are studying art, you may wish to use your artistic skills to undertake the role of designer. Or, if you have a knowledge of a particular period of history, you may wish to direct a play set in that time.

ONLINE TEST

Test yourself on the roles and responsibilities involved in CfE Higher Drama at www.brightredbooks.net

MORE ROLES AND RESPONSIBILITIES

SET DESIGN

A set designer must be creative and have a wide-ranging set of skills. He or she must be able to interpret the text and the director's ideas, and communicate these through the various stages of design – from initial sketches and mood boards, to drawing elevations and plans, and constructing the final set. A set designer usually works closely with the props master, as these two areas must enhance and support each other to create a coherent visual image onstage.

Responsibilities

- Discuss the interpretation of the text and its impact on the set.
- Echo the mood and atmosphere of the text in the design.
- Check what resources are available.
- Source materials.
- Understand and create a set that is suitable to the venue.
- Liaise with costume, lighting, props, and the stage manager and director to ensure the mood created is consistent.
- Build a scale model of the set and provide a rehearsal set (this is not required at Higher Level).
- Oversee the building of the set and how it is laid out.

ONLINE

Visit the website of your local theatre. Most theatres have 'who's who' lists which detail the names and e-mail addresses of people who fulfil the various production roles. If you would like to know more about a particular production role, why not e-mail someone who does the job in reality and ask for any advice or words of wisdom. Many theatres also have video interviews with various members of the team which may give you more of an insight into what the job actually entails.

PROPS

There is a crossover between props and both set and costume design. Communication is very important in this role, as the props provided must complement these other areas and help to communicate the time/place setting and moods, atmospheres and tensions of the play.

Responsibilities

- Study the text to discover what props must be sourced.
- Identify **personal** and **set props**.
- Liaise with the director, set designer and lighting designer to ensure that props are appropriate.
- Consider health and safety implications.
- Source props, whether in the store, borrowed, purchased or made.
- Consider weight, shape, size and durability of props.
- Create and keep a **props table**, checking before, during and after each performance that all props required are present.
- Create a props cue sheet so that stage management is aware of what is required and when.
- Repair damaged props.
- Return and store props.

COSTUME

Costume is vital in communicating the themes and issues of a production, as well as the time and place setting and aspects of the characters' personalities. In this role, you will work closely with the make-up and hair and props people, as the different roles must complement each other. This is a very creative role and it is beneficial if the costume designer has some artistic flair in order to be able to communicate ideas visually.

Responsibilities

- Research the setting of the drama, the time and place.
- Liaise with the director, and the lighting and set designers, to create the required mood and atmosphere.
- Work within a budget and to a time scale.
- Read the play carefully to find textual references to costume.
- Discover what is available within the wardrobe, and what needs to be sourced through purchasing, making, altering and borrowing.
- Have a detailed knowledge of the characters and how the director interprets them in order to design their costume.

MAKE-UP AND HAIR

Make-up and hair are crucial to enhancing characterisation and communicating meaning to an audience. A make-up designer must reflect the setting of the play and use his or her skills to assist the actors in developing their characters. A make-up and hair specialist will work closely with the costume designer and lighting designer to ensure that the detail can be seen clearly by the audience and that it complements the costume design.

Responsibilities

- Work closely with the costume designer to create the appropriate look for characters.
- Research the setting of the text and source materials.
- List characters' make-up requirements and make sketches for make-up artists/actors to follow.
- Follow health and safety guidelines: for example, checking ingredients for allergies and performing patch tests.
- Clean and store make-up and hair products appropriately.
- Oversee the application of make-up for performance and ensure it is effective.

 DON'T FORGET

In the practical exam, you can specialise in either acting, directing or design. If you choose design, you must specialise in **set design** and **one** other supplementary area from lighting, sound, props, costume, make-up and hair.

 **THINGS TO DO AND THINK ABOUT**

Consider the different responsibilities of the roles detailed on these pages. Are there any areas you think you would be suitable for? To assess which area you could specialise in, make a list of personal points and qualities which you possess and look at these side by side with the roles you are interested in.

 ONLINE TEST

Test yourself on the roles and responsibilities involved in CfE Higher Drama at www.brightredbooks.net

ACTING — PREPARATION

An actor is responsible for communicating his or her role and the content of the production to an audience. Actors are the playwright's and director's voice, and the success of a production can firmly rest on their performance. In the next few pages, we will explore the requirements of the role and how you can prepare to fulfil your responsibilities as an actor to a high standard.

RESEARCH

As with directing or design, it is imperative that you thoroughly research the play and the role you are going to portray. You should conduct some initial research into the play you are going to perform and find out as much information as you can about its context, setting, themes and issues (see the section on research in Directing – Pre-Rehearsal, page 36). Further to this initial research, you can also find out more about the character you are going to portray. The following questions are designed to help you do this.

- Is the character based on a real person?
- How have other people interpreted the role?
- Are there any physical elements which will help the portrayal of the character?
- What does the character look like?

ONLINE

A great way of finding out about the character is to conduct an image search online. This will give you a good idea of how the character has been portrayed by others and may also lead you to clips of past productions.

INTERPRETATION

After you have gained information about the play and your character, you can begin to interpret this character in your own way. To do this, you must study the text very closely, not only what your own character does and says, but also what other characters say about your character or how they react when your character is present. Equipped with your research into the play and the character you are playing, you should be in a good position to develop your own interpretation. To assist you with this, you may wish to carry out some individual characterisation work. Below are some examples of tasks you could undertake to begin to develop your interpretation.

Character iceberg

An iceberg only has 20 per cent of its mass above the water level and this could also be true of a theatrical character. When you create a **character iceberg** above the water line, you note down facts about the character – things you know to be true from the text and your research. Underneath the water line you should note down information that you have interpreted or decided upon.

Role on the wall

Like a character iceberg, '**role on the wall**' is about the outer and inner character. Draw an outline of a figure and, around the figure, make notes on how the character is seen by others. Inside the outline, note down internal aspects of the character.

Character profile

A **character profile** is a detailed record of the character you are portraying. In a character profile, you should include as much detail as possible about the character (which can be factual, such as name and age, and interpretative, such as personality). A character profile is a working document and can be added to and altered throughout the rehearsal process. You could use the following headings to create a detailed character profile:

- Name, age, occupation
- Personality
- Background
- Relationships
- Hobbies and interests
- Likes/dislikes
- **Status**
- Motivation
- Objectives

Character analysis questions

The legendary acting teacher and theatre practitioner Uta Hagen approached detailed character analysis through the use of questions. Uta Hagen's nine questions are an excellent place to start in your preparation for performing your acting role. Many actors use these, but the list of possible questions which you should be able to answer for your character is almost endless. An overview of the nine questions is provided here:

1   Who am I? – Who is the character at the beginning of the play/scene and who are they by the end?

2   Where am I? – Environment, location, conditions, physiological and mental state.

3   What surrounds me? – Persons, objects (colour and texture).

4   What time is it? – Hour, minute, date, year, century, era.

5   What are the given circumstances? – Those events, facts, and conditions occurring before or during the play/scene that affect the character and/or action.

6   What is my relationship? – To all of the above and to other characters is it solid or shifting?

7   What do I want? – Objectives or intention: includes the overall character objectives as well as more immediate beat-to-beat intentions.

8   What's in my way? – Obstacles, people, actions, events.

9   What do I do to get what I want? – Throughout the play/scene what does the character do to achieve their goals?

(Adapted from Uta Hagen, *Respect for Acting*)

Although these are excellent questions for getting you to think about your character, you may wish to come up with your own supplementary questions to deepen your understanding of them.

Role on the Wall

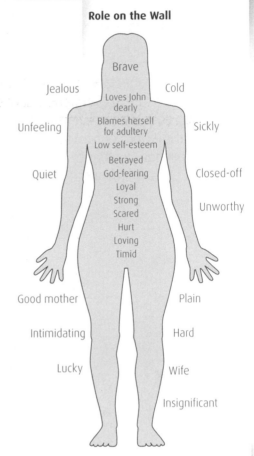

Brave
Jealous
Cold
Loves John dearly
Blames herself for adultery
Low self-esteem
Unfeeling
Sickly
Betrayed
God-fearing
Quiet
Closed-off
Loyal
Strong
Unworthy
Scared
Hurt
Loving
Timid
Good mother
Plain
Intimidating
Hard
Lucky
Wife
Insignificant

Elizabeth Proctor – *The Crucible*

 ONLINE

To find out more about Uta Hagen and the nine questions, head to www.brightredbooks.net

 DON'T FORGET

Although you have a number of ideas for how you will interpret your character, they may not marry with the ideas of your fellow actors or director. For the good of the production as a whole, it is important to remain adaptable and not be too heavily rooted in your interpretation.

 THINGS TO DO AND THINK ABOUT

Try out some of the exercises above (or some of your own) to develop your character, and make a list of how you could show these traits in performance through your use of voice, movement and characterisation.

 ONLINE TEST

Test yourself on preparing for acting at www.brightredbooks.net

ACTING — REHEARSAL AND PERFORMANCE

During the rehearsal process, you will work collaboratively with your fellow actors, director and designer. At this point in your drama career you will be familiar with the rehearsal process and how to develop an acting role for performance. However, at a higher level you are expected to be responsible for your own progress and should be able to work alone or with other students under your teacher's guidance. The main point is that you are a generous and well-mannered actor, which can be difficult at times, especially when the performance date gets closer.

ACTING DOS AND DON'TS IN REHEARSAL

Do

- Be 'off book'. Learn your lines at the earliest possible opportunity. It is difficult to fully inhabit a character if you are reading from a script, and your movement should not be constrained by having a book in your hand.

- Note down all your blocking. You should be self-sufficient in knowing where you should be and what you should be doing at any given point in a scene. Don't rely on your memory – it will fail you and your director will become irritated!

- Warm up before the rehearsal. This will prevent you from becoming tired and distracted or straining your voice during intensive dialogue.

- Rehearse as if it is a performance. You should give one hundred per cent effort to all rehearsals.

- Take risks in rehearsal. Experiment and try things out.

- Be ready for your entrance. Don't wait for someone to tell you to enter stage right. If you have it noted in your blocking, be ready to do it.

- Use rehearsal 'downtime' when you aren't onstage to study your text, learn your lines and blocking and watch your fellow actors. You can learn from both their successes and their mistakes.

- Be punctual and prepared for rehearsals. If you have been given notes to work on, ensure you do this in preparation for the next rehearsal.

- Take notes throughout rehearsals.

contd

Don't

- Expect the director to have all the answers. Creating theatre is the most collaborative of art forms and you must ensure you come to rehearsals armed with ideas and concepts to demonstrate practically in rehearsal.

- Take things personally. Criticism is constructive and designed to make your performance better.

- Change what you do onstage without rehearsing it first. This could put your fellow actors off or cause cues to be missed.

- Criticise other actors' performances as this could cause resentments.

- Talk when not involved in the rehearsal action.

- Expect everyone to agree with you all of the time. Approach any disagreements constructively and courteously and resolve issues quickly.

REFINEMENT AND DEVELOPMENT

It is difficult to outline all the activities an actor will be involved in during the main body of rehearsals. It may be that particular moments need close and focused work, and further workshop sessions may be required to get things right. You will mainly be involved in rehearsals, character development and learning your lines and cues. It is important that you continually evaluate your progress and work out how you can improve. Have open dialogues throughout this process with your director, designer and other actors to ensure you are all 'singing from the same hymn sheet'. You must be self-disciplined and motivated throughout the development process.

FINAL PRESENTATION

Your final presentation is effectively your performance. However, you must also be able to discuss your character and how you will portray the character through either a written format or in discussion. To do this, you should continue to make detailed notes on your characterisation, voice and movement choices and then demonstrate these choices in performance. You should also complete detailed character outlines which can be presented as **character cards**, 'role on the wall', icebergs or any other appropriate format.

THINGS TO DO AND THINK ABOUT

When taking on an acting role, it is quite easy to get caught up in the practical elements of the specialism. You must ensure that you are keeping a note of how you have developed the character throughout the rehearsal process. This should also be evident in your final performance of the role.

 **DON'T FORGET**

Warm up! Before any theatrical performance, it is important that an actor is fully in tune with the character they are portraying and is physically and vocally prepared for the performance. To do this, you should develop a warm-up routine which is specific and focused.

 VIDEO LINK

Watch actors warming up at www.brightredbooks.net

 ONLINE TEST

Test yourself on this topic online at www.brightredbooks.net

DIRECTING — PRE-REHEARSAL

The role of the director is pivotal to the success of any theatrical production. As a director, you will be responsible for making decisions which affect all of the other roles in the production. The idea that a director should be all-powerful and should dictate to the actors and crew how to achieve his or her artistic vision is somewhat outdated. To be a good director, above all else, you must be a good negotiator and you must be able to compromise your ideals for the good of the production where necessary. All the production team must have input in terms of their ideas for design and characterisation, for example. It is up to a good director to recognise their team's strengths, and to harness and channel them into the production.

THE DIRECTOR'S RESPONSIBILITIES

As a director, you will have responsibility for initiating, developing and coordinating all areas of the production. You will plan a schedule and engage with your designer in the pre-production stage. You will cast your actors and plan and communicate your ideas for blocking, characterisation, voice and movement. You must be able to negotiate and communicate clearly with your team to lead them 'from page to stage' – from the original textual extract to the performance. Following the performance, you will engage in an evaluation of how you and your team have worked together to realise the production.

PLANNING

The adage 'Failing to prepare is preparing to fail' is totally true in the case of directing a play. Before you have had your initial production meeting with your cast and crew, you must have a clear vision and expectations for the final performance. You must be able to communicate your plans clearly at the outset of the process, as once rehearsals are under way your energies as director will probably be focused on your actors, and the designers will be left to work on their own initiative to develop ideas for your approval.

Research

Initial research is essential in gaining an understanding of the text you are staging. There may well be aspects of the play or the actions of its characters that do not make sense to you on first reading. By researching the play and rereading it from different characters' perspectives, you should be able to fully understand and interpret the play.

Areas to research:

- The historical setting
- The geographical setting
- Politics
- **Social context**

- Popular culture (music, cinema, television, hobbies and pasttimes)
- The playwright – his/her other work, status, popularity
- Themes/issues/messages of the text

Following your initial research, you can utilise what you have learned to inform your interpretation and performance concepts.

Marking your script

Before you start the rehearsal process, as director, you should begin to mark your blocking on the text. This gives essential information such as entrances and exits, moves and positioning for your actors. Your blocking should be flexible and, through negotiation

contd

with your actors (they will have ideas too), you may wish to alter and adapt as you go. Throughout your rehearsal period, you may also wish to construct a dramatic commentary which will allow you to demonstrate your blocking and interpretative notes alongside your chosen technical effects and justification of your choices. This will be a clear demonstration of your understanding and interpretation of the text and a great addition to your folio.

Dramatic commentary

Annotating the text – Through the numbering of particular words and lines on your script, you can clearly link them to the columns on the dramatic commentary. This will make it obvious and easy to follow your instructions.

Moves and interpretative notes – In this column, you should cross-reference your explanation with the script (through your numbered annotations). Here, you should detail the actors' entrances and exits, their movements (**facial expression**, **body language**, etc.) and their moves across stage and how they are to carry them out: for example, *Parris x's (crosses) DSR (Down Stage Right) at a fast pace*. In addition to this, you should detail any voice instruction, proxemics and positioning plus any other interpretative notes.

Justification – Again, through cross-referencing, you should explain why you have chosen to direct your actors in a particular way: for example, *to show he is angry at Abigail's lack of respect*.

Effects – In the final column of the commentary, you should explain any lighting (LFX), sound (SFX) and special effects that are essential to the action.

Example:

Extract from dramatic commentary

MERCUTIO	(1)	Where the devil should this Romeo be? Came he not home to-night?
BENVOLIO		Not to his father's; I spoke with his man.
MERCUTIO	(2)	Ah, that same pale hard-hearted wench, that Rosaline. Torments him so, that he will sure run mad.
BENVOLIO		Tybalt, the kinsman of old Capulet, (LFX 2) Hath sent a letter to his father's house.

Moves and interpretative notes	Justification	Technical effects
(1) M enters USR and x's DSC at a quick pace with a flustered tone and aggravated facial expression.	He is in a hurry to find Romeo as he has not seen him since the previous night. He is an emotional character and is quite rash and over the top.	LFX 2: On the mention of Tybalt's letter the lights fade to a lower intensity to signify that this is not a positive event.
(2) M laughs and shakes his head.	Rosaline has been giving Romeo the run-around for a while and M finds it amusing that Romeo still lusts after her.	

Through careful planning and research, a director can set the whole production up for success. It makes it much easier to communicate what you want to see in performance if you have detailed notes and plans to work from.

 VIDEO LINK

Check out the clip at www.brightredbooks.net for expert advice on how to direct a play.

 DON'T FORGET

By photocopying your script pages and sticking them to A4 paper or into a workbook, you will have much more 'white space' around the lines of the text to write your notes. You can also place a blank page opposite each page of script in order to write notes, lists and diagrams – displaying your thought processes and serving as a reminder to you during rehearsals. Be sure to check the copyright licence with your teacher before photocopying.

THINGS TO DO AND THINK ABOUT

List, list, list!

Lists are the director's friend. They are essential for keeping organised and developing the text for performance. Read through the extract you are planning to direct. Using different coloured pens or pencils, note down anything that the extract requires, such as a character's entrance, a personal prop, or a lighting change. Ask yourself if there is anything else which is ESSENTIAL to the performance of the extract and list it! This will help you keep your team on track and enable you to clearly communicate your ideas and vision to all concerned.

 ONLINE TEST

Test yourself on directing at www.brightredbooks.net

DIRECTING — CASTING

The director is key to the success of any theatrical production. It can, at times, be a lonely and stressful job, as the entire team looks to you for help and guidance and you must be extremely organised and lead by example. But, it is a very rewarding role; it's a wonderful feeling to see what you imagined come to fruition in performance. This section will explore the process of casting and how the director leads this process.

CASTING

Casting is the process by which the director determines who will play each role. This is a crucial part of the directing process. Once you have cast the actors, it would be quite unfair to change their roles, unless there is a pressing reason to do so, such as an actor in a lead role missing too many rehearsals. Even though you will probably know your actors very well by the time you come to cast them, it is still important that you complete some sort of **audition** process to avoid typecasting, as someone you may not have thought of could surprise you. The audition doesn't have to be a daunting experience for your actors and it is important that you make them feel as comfortable as possible in order to get the best possible performance from them. There are different approaches to auditioning, and you should explore your options before deciding on what will suit both yourself and the actors you are working with.

Audition workshop

If you choose to use the workshop format, you will look at the themes and issues and character requirements of your chosen text and plan your workshop around them. You can then devise activities which require your actors to improvise and portray aspects of the play and its characters. This will allow you to ascertain who will suit each role in the play without the pressure of sight reading. For example, if you were auditioning for *Romeo and Juliet* you might ask your cast to improvise a romantic or tragic situation, taking on specific character attributes, such as the dreamer, the devious, the confrontational, etc.

DON'T FORGET

Although you won't necessarily have a formal audition where you decide the roles your actors will play, this is the usual process for casting for larger school or youth theatre productions, and it is the norm in the professional theatre. You may wish to use some of the examples in your first rehearsal.

contd

Performing a scene

You may choose to give your actors a specific scene to perform. If you choose this method, it is important that you provide them with a clear understanding of how you see the scene/characters being performed, in addition to allowing your actors some scope to demonstrate their own interpretation of the role. They may surprise you with something that you hadn't thought of but that is really effective.

A read-through

This is more pressurised for your actors; however, if you give them notes as they read the character aloud, you can gain a good understanding of how each actor responds to your direction and if that will benefit their portrayal of the character. You can also switch roles as they read, so that they're effectively auditioning for all the roles at the same time.

Whichever approach you choose, or whether you use a combination of all of them, it is important that you take notes or record the auditions, as you may wish to reflect on them before making your final decision on casting.

Below is an example casting workshop format which includes a variety of the approaches detailed above.

Example:

Ice breaker – Princesses and Pirates. Nothing lowers people's inhibitions like a good old-fashioned game of tig. In this variation of tunnel tig, the 'pirate' or chaser has to tag as many 'princesses' as possible. If tagged, the princess must stand on the spot waving their hands in the air, shouting 'help me, help me', and they can be released by another princess taking their hands and jumping on the spot.

Improvisation – The cast are split into pairs and named A and B. A has the objective of keeping a secret, while B has to try to uncover the truth. The scene is set in a church. This improvisation helps the director see how the actors react in a situation and which character traits they adopt that are similar to the characters being cast.

Scene – Lastly, the actors are given a short extract from the play. The director explains how he/she sees each of the characters and gives the actors time to rehearse the scene. After each pair performs the scene to the director, they are given some notes and asked to repeat the scene again. This allows the director to gauge how the actors react to advice and who can understand and portray which character according to the director's vision.

DON'T FORGET

It is the director's job to communicate clearly with his or her actors to ensure they are comfortable and happy during the casting process.

 ONLINE

Have a look at the blog at www.brightredbooks.net to get some ideas and advice on what to do and not to do in an audition.

 THINGS TO DO AND THINK ABOUT

Plan your audition. Think about what activities you could do to break the ice, and structure your audition with the needs of your chosen play and its characters in mind.

 ONLINE TEST

Test yourself on the casting process at www.brightredbooks.net

DIRECTING — REHEARSALS

During early rehearsals, your planning and listing really come to the fore. Your initial ideas may change and develop during this phase of the process, so it is vital that you do not become too fixed in your concepts at this stage. However, you should still maintain a clear vision of what you wish to achieve. During this period of rehearsals, you should be able to action and block your extract from the play, in addition to beginning to develop characters and convey meaning.

ACTIONING

This is the process of breaking down your chosen extract into actions or sections. These sections should be split in terms of changes in mood/ atmosphere, entrances and exits, or events. Breaking your extract down should help you to focus on specific moments, and to organise and plan your rehearsals.

BLOCKING

This is the process of deciding where and when characters move onstage. This seems simple enough, but what you have planned and the reality of seeing the play 'up' may not marry. If you do alter any moves or positions during the process of blocking, you must be sure to mark it on your copy of the script so that they are maintained in later rehearsals. It is also vital that you make sure your actors mark their moves on their scripts so that they can learn them as they learn their lines. When communicating with other members of the production team, it is essential that your blocking is clearly noted to ensure that they know what you need them to create. During this process, you may also wish to start using a rehearsal set, props and costume, as these will influence how your actors move and communicate meaning. For example, if you were directing a period piece such as *A Doll's House*, you might want your female actors to wear full-length skirts.

DON'T FORGET

Record any changes in your blocking on your script. You can also write any production notes/ cues etc. as and when they should happen.

DEPTH AND DETAIL

Once you have blocked your extract and the actors have begun to learn their lines, it is time to add depth and detail to the performance and the characters portrayed. You may undertake character development tasks during this stage of the process, such as hot seating. The most important thing for a director to do during the development of the performance is to watch and listen to everything that goes on, both onstage and off – for example, as the actors are discussing things between themselves. Take notes and develop 'rehearsal memory' so that you know not only the blocking of a scene but also the thinking and feelings behind it.

BUSINESS

As you add depth and detail to your scenes, your actors should begin to inhabit more fully the characters they portray. You can guide, or be guided by, your actors as they develop 'business' for their characters. This could be how they interact with the other characters (for example, touching a shoulder or holding hands), how they interact with the set and props (for example, picking up a picture, drumming their fingers on a desk), or how they develop **mannerisms** and **gestures** for their character (for example, twirling their hair, wringing their hands). This 'business' may be imposed by the text or could naturally develop as you rehearse.

PRODUCTION MEETINGS

Throughout the rehearsal process, the director mainly focuses on the actors and their **interactions** onstage. However, it is vital that you also make time to interact with the other production areas and keep them up to date on developments and specific tasks that need to be carried out. The director usually leads these meetings, but it is the designer's chance to present his or her ideas to the director and to get feedback on progress and any problems that have been encountered.

TECHNICAL AND DRESS REHEARSALS

At this stage, all aspects of the performance begin to come together. It is the director's chance to see what the production will look and feel like in performance. It is useful to have a separate technical rehearsal so that everyone can ensure they know the cues for lighting, sound and set changes. This rehearsal can be led jointly by the director and the technicians as it is predominantly for their benefit. The dress rehearsal will give the costume and make-up and hair people the opportunity to check that their creations are fit for purpose, and that they are aware of any quick changes. The actors also benefit hugely from a well-run dress rehearsal, as they begin to see themselves as the character and are able to communicate this more strongly.

OFFERING FEEDBACK

During and after rehearsals, the director should offer feedback for the actors and designer. When offering feedback, it is important to be constructive and to be careful not to offend the people you are working with. A good way to achieve this is to offer both positive and negative notes for your actors and production team so that everyone feels valued and can positively address any changes they need to make.

 THINGS TO DO AND THINK ABOUT

If you can, film some of your rehearsals – particularly your dress rehearsal. This will help highlight any issues to your actors and designer in addition to helping you to reflect on the progress of your piece.

 ONLINE

Check out the link at www.brightredbooks.net for more details of the blocking and rehearsal process.

 ONLINE TEST

Test yourself on the rehearsal stage of directing at www.brightredbooks.net

DESIGN — SET DESIGN

A designer in the theatre works in a very similar way to a director. A designer oversees all the technical people and must guide and lead them through the rehearsal and production process. It is recognised that in most school situations having a designer and team of technicians is not likely to be possible. Throughout the production unit, you will explore different production areas and gain an understanding of each. If you choose design for the final exam, you will specialise in two areas, one of which must be set design. In the following section, we will explore set design in detail, what activities you may choose to undertake and how you can demonstrate a sound theatrical set design concept throughout the rehearsal process and in performance.

ONLINE

An excellent example of how set design can communicate with the audience is from *Mary Queen of Scots Got Her Head Chopped Off* performed at The Lyceum Theatre, Edinburgh in 2011. Have a look at the production at www.brightredbooks.net

WHAT MAKES A GOOD SET DESIGNER?

A good set designer must have excellent communication skills, the ability to work on his or her own initiative, **creativity**, and the ability to learn new skills, adapt to new situations, and problem-solve. When creating a set design, there are three key questions for a set designer to ask during each stage of the process.

Does it help the actors?

There is no point in having a set that is aesthetically pleasing if it pulls focus from the action and the actors within the production. If the set design hinders the actors' movement or the audience's sight lines, the whole production will fall flat. The designer's job is to support the actors and enhance their performance.

Does it communicate meaning?

The set can be the audience's first clue about the setting of the drama. It can be used to highlight where and when the play is set, in addition to creating mood and atmosphere and tension. A strong set design concept can also help highlight a central theme, issue or metaphor.

How can I create it?

By considering the materials that can be used, how much they might cost and if there are the resources to create the design, the designer must try to communicate how his or her concepts would work in reality, with a clear plan of how it can be created. This can then be discussed with the director and cast before the set is actually constructed. It is important to note that, when specialising in set design for the Production Skills unit, the set must be constructed using available resources. For the course assessment, the set design must be clear through, for example, ground plans, but it does not need to be fully constructed.

PRE-PRODUCTION

Initially, you must research the text to be performed and consider, through discussions with your director, what the requirements of your set design will be. You must then begin to develop possible ideas and concepts which could be developed into a performance concept. These must be communicated clearly so that all parties involved have a definite view of what to expect from your design. It is important that you can communicate your initial ideas both orally and pictorially so that everyone is able to visualise what the finished set will look like. There are a variety of ways of doing this, some of which are described on the following page.

contd

Mind-maps and concept maps

As with any creative endeavour, this is a good place to start. Following on from an initial mind-map, you may wish to develop a concept map, to explore possible ways to communicate a particular theme, issue or metaphor through aspects of your design, such as set dressing, furniture, colour, texture and materials. This will help you to focus on particular areas in detail and explain them to others.

Mood boards

You may decide on a particular colour, mood or theme. Mood boards can help you develop these concepts, in addition to enabling you to communicate your ideas visually with others. On a mood board you can include photographs, materials, notes, sketches, colours, etc.

Sketches

You can create rough sketches to help you understand how things can fit together, and to visualise how your ideas will work and how busy your set will be in terms of furniture, set, backdrops, etc.

Ground plans

These are essential in helping you fit your set together. Much needs to be considered when creating a ground plan, and at this stage you should create several to give yourself options on what you can include and where it should be positioned. (See page 45 for more about ground plans.)

Elevations

Elevations are technical drawings which are drawn to scale and can provide a representation of what the set will look like in 3D. In the early stages, these can be created to a rough scale; however, when it comes to the final design you need to be more accurate.

To model or not to model

At Higher level it is not a requirement that you create a set model; however, creating a set model may support you, your director and the actors. A set model does not need to be high-spec – a simple 'shoebox set' may be all that is needed in the early stages.

REHEARSAL AND PERFORMANCE

Once you have presented and discussed your design concepts with the director and cast, you will need to work quickly to provide them with a rehearsal set, so that any problems or issues can be identified and tackled early. A rehearsal set could simply be tables, chairs and **rostra** positioned to illustrate the whereabouts of different items. You may also wish to use masking tape to highlight exits and entrances, and any positions or 'black spots' where an actor would be hidden by an item on set. This will help the director and actors block the play and avoid unnecessary problems later. While they are busy rehearsing, you can focus on fine-tuning and developing your design before pulling it all together for the final performance.

DON'T FORGET

There is no requirement to create a set model for Higher Drama, but you may find it useful to work from.

DON'T FORGET

Arrange times to meet with your director and discuss how the design is progressing. This could be in production meetings or at other points when required. Tackling issues early will pay off in the final performance.

 THINGS TO DO AND THINK ABOUT

It is important that you do not wait to be told what to do by your director, but develop your ideas straight away. Try using some of the example activities above and present your ideas back at the earliest opportunity to avoid issues at a later stage.

 ONLINE TEST

Test yourself on set design at www.brightredbooks.net

SET DESIGN — TECHNICAL ASPECTS OF DESIGN

Designing a set is a creative process. It is also a technical one, and planning and practice are key to ensuring that your design functions in performance. From the very outset of the process, you must pay close attention to technical opportunities and constraints, and develop ways of working with them rather than against them.

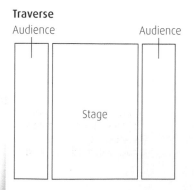

PERFORMANCE SPACE

You may be lucky enough to have access to a variety of performance spaces within your school or college, but be aware that you may have restricted access if it is not your usual drama space. Whichever space your piece will be performed in, you have an element of choice about how your stage will be configured. There are positive and negative aspects to each theatre shape, and you must assess these in addition to weighing up whether they would have a positive or negative impact on your production concept and the performance overall.

- **End on/proscenium arch** – This is probably the most common staging style in drama studios and school theatres. Sight lines are usually easy to manage, you can often use backdrops or projections to enhance the mood and atmosphere, and the actors have clear entrances and exits. However, the audience can feel removed from the action because of the effect of the '**fourth wall**'.

Four types of stage

Proscenium arch

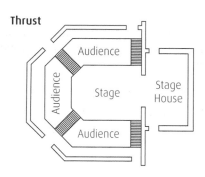

- **Traverse** – In this configuration, you can place scenic design at either end, and if you have an interesting concept for using the floor of the acting area to enhance mood and atmosphere this may be a good choice. Sight lines can be an issue and lighting can also be difficult to **focus** without blinding part of the audience!

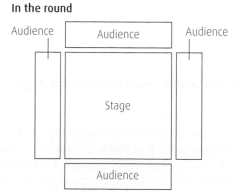

- **Thrust** – This could be seen as the happy medium, as you can still use the back wall of the staging area, in addition to having your actors come into the audience more via the thrust. This staging breaks the 'fourth wall', but again sight lines and lighting can be an issue.

 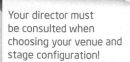
- **Theatre in the round** – This staging can be really effective in creating an intimate atmosphere or, if your audience is raised and looking down on the action, an intimidating mood. There are problems with entrances and exits here, which could be avoided by using vomitoria (the audience entrance corridors in a theatre). In addition, there are, again, issues with sight lines and lighting.

- **Site-specific** – If you choose to set your production in a site-specific location, it could greatly enhance your communication of the location, themes and issues of the play. However, you will have to deal with the constraints of weather, if outdoors, as well as technical issues, lack of lighting or acoustic problems.

TECHNICAL DRAWINGS

Ground plans

Ground plans are vital for ensuring that you, the director, cast and crew are all fully aware of where items should be and how they should be positioned. There are particular terms and symbols relating to ground plans, which all the relevant people must understand. They should be drawn to scale. Professional designers use a 1:25 scale for ground plans and set models. 1 cm on the plan equates to 25 cm on the acting area (so if the stage is 6 metres wide it is 24 cm wide on the plan). A ground plan must be clear and easy to follow, and it is the basis for other technical drawings produced later on (elevations). Below is a step-by-step guide to drawing an accurate ground plan.

1 Measure your acting area and work out your scale. Use a measuring tape or measuring wheel, and be as accurate as you can in measuring the depth and width of the performance space. You then need to work out your scale – it is possible to buy or borrow 1:25 rulers which may help you to complete the ground plan, or you can calculate this fairly simply.

2 Add a clear title to the upper left-hand corner of the page which indicates the play, scene, location and scale.

3 Draw the outline of your acting area. Using a ruler, accurately draw out the 'walls' of your acting area. Following this, add a centre line, which is a broken line going from top to bottom of your page.

4 Add the position of the audience.

5 Add any fixed items, **backdrops**, **cyclorama**, door **flats**, etc. using the appropriate symbols.

6 This then becomes your master copy. If you are using multiple sets where different items are brought on or off stage, you can use tracing paper or acetates and create a layered document which shows each scene.

7 Measure any other non-fixed set and furniture and apply the same scale – 1:25.

8 Once you have completed the ground plan for each scene, you can check the audience's sight lines by choosing different positions and sketching pencil lines across the page.

Elevations

Now that you have completed the ground plan, you can use and apply your measurements and scale to draw a front elevation of your set. This is basically a pictorial description of what your set will look like from the audience's perspective. Depending on which **stage configuration** you are using, you may need to do several elevations of each scene so that you have a clear idea of how your set will look from each angle.

Set model

If you choose to, you can use the same measurements to create a scale set model. In addition to the measurements you already have, you will also need to know how high the walls are and include this in your model. The best material to use for a set model is foamboard, but if that is not available then stiff card should suffice.

 ONLINE

The link at www.brightredbooks.net should remind you how to work out ratios!

 DON'T FORGET

At Higher Drama level you do not have to construct the full performance set. However, it is useful to enhance your rehearsal set by adding set dressing and any scenery you can source, as it will assist your actors and the audience in their understanding of the play.

 ONLINE

More information on how to create a set model can be found at www.brightredbooks.netl

 THINGS TO DO AND THINK ABOUT

Make a plan!

At the outset, the process of designing a set may seem fairly straightforward. However, as we have seen, the technical requirements in terms of planning and communication concepts are fairly taxing. Knowing the play you are going to design for, create a to-do list, taking into account the technical requirements of the role.

 ONLINE TEST

Test yourself on set design at www.brightredbooks.net

DESIGN — PROPS

Props or properties are an integral part of a theatrical production. They add realism to a piece of theatre, and can enhance the action and communicate meaning to an audience. For a production to be believable and its actors to be believed, the appropriate props must be in place in order to conduct 'business' and carry out the requirements of the text. Props are also important when being used as set dressing, as this has a pivotal role in communicating the setting and meaning of the production. To carry out a props role as part of the Higher Drama course, there are certain tasks you must undertake in order to be successful. As with any role, you must first conduct research and develop your own interpretation of the text. If you are specialising in props for the final exam, you will link your props design with the set design. If you are doing props as part of your Production Skills unit, you must liaise closely with the set designer and costume designer to ensure there are strong links between each area.

DON'T FORGET

As part of the Production Skills unit assessment, all props must be sourced or adapted. For the final exam you should make at least one prop.

REHEARSAL AND PRODUCTION

Pre-production

Initially, the job of a props designer is to list and plan. You should read the text, highlighting any key props that are required. You should then list these and mind-map/concept-map each prop required, noting down whether it is to be:

- **sourced** – from your drama department or from home, or borrowed or purchased from elsewhere

- **adapted** – altered in some way, painted, embellished, aged etc., to make it more suitable for the play being performed

- **made** – if you cannot find an appropriate prop or one that can be adapted, you may have to make it from scratch.

As with set design, you may wish to create mood boards initially to help display your ideas and concepts. You should then begin to develop these ideas through sketches and photographs, and annotate them to explain to your director and cast exactly what will be used in performance. If you are working on creating props during rehearsal, it may be necessary to provide your actors with rehearsal props to use so that they have a feel for what they will have in performance.

contd

War Horse

During rehearsal

In the run-up to the performance, you should be gathering your props together and altering, mending, adapting and making them as required. You must also clearly label props and create an inventory listing each item, as well as storing them all appropriately. The following gives some guidance on how you could go about this and the evidence you should create throughout the process.

Props list – You should split your list into three columns: personal or hand props, set props and **costume props**. Each column should then be split into the scenes/sections being performed. You can then list all the required props in their suitable place, making it very easy to manage and use at a glance.

Props table – You will need a fairly large table for this so that you can lay your props out and clearly label them. It is a good idea to use masking tape to section the table into squares for each prop. You may also choose to label each with the name of the prop that should be kept there, so that it is always easy to see at a glance if there is anything missing.

Labelling – Labelling is very important, particularly if you have similar props or several actors using the same thing. Labelling should ensure that it is returned safely each time it is used or, if you have several identical props to be used by several characters, that each actor has his or her own allocated prop. It is good practice, if possible, to label each square on your table in addition to each prop. You could even colour code your props to correspond with your props list – personal prop green, set prop blue and costume prop red, for example. Small coloured dots would suffice, or you could use stickers to make the colours removable.

Adapted prop – It could be that the prop you have sourced is not quite right. You may need to change its colour or embellish it in some way. You may have permission to alter it permanently or it may have to be a temporary measure. You need to be creative here and consider the materials available. Painting items is the simplest approach, but covering with fabric or paper may be just as effective, and using masking tape to attach items is less permanent than glue. Consider all of your options before fixing on one solution, and experiment to reach a suitable outcome.

The made prop – Trying to come up with a prop to make, or how to make it, can be quite daunting. The prop itself does not need to be complicated, but it must be robust enough to be worked with in both rehearsal and performance (it may be useful to make a few so that you have a back-up if one gets damaged). The prop needs to be simple enough for you to create and make it yourself – this will vary according to your own skill set – but complex enough to be an interesting prop to create, and to allow your creativity to shine through.

ONLINE

Learn more about props by following the link at www.brightredbooks.net

 THINGS TO DO AND THINK ABOUT

Get organised!

A props designer/master has to be super-organised in order to avoid things going missing or getting damaged. Be firm but fair with the actors using your props; list and label everything meticulously; and wherever possible create a back-up. This will avoid problems later on.

 ONLINE TEST

Test yourself on designing props at www.brightredbooks.net

DESIGN — COSTUME 1

As with props and set designers, costume designers must be proficient communicators. The design process is collaborative and you must have a shared view among the director, cast and designers in order for the production to be successful. Costume plays a vital role in communicating the context of the piece, its themes, issues, genre and style and, perhaps most important, the personalities of its characters. A well-researched and designed costume can really enhance an actor's performance and is vital in helping the actor communicate with the audience. In order to be a successful costume designer, you must be creative and organised. There are a number of tasks and duties which you should carry out to progress and evidence the development of your costume design.

PRE-PRODUCTION

DON'T FORGET

For the Production Skills unit you must adapt at least one costume and source all other costumes. For the course assessment you should make the costume, or adapt it extensively, and source/ adapt all other costumes.

Initially, the job of a costume designer is to list and plan. You should read the text, highlighting any key items of costume and any character points or descriptions that are required. You should then list these and mind-map/concept-map each element of costume required, noting down whether it is to be:

- **sourced** – from your drama department or from home, or borrowed or purchased from elsewhere

- **adapted** – altered in some way, embellished, dyed, taken in or let out, to make it more suitable for the play being performed

- **made** – if you cannot find an appropriate costume or one that can be adapted, you may have to make it from scratch.

As with set design and props, you may wish to create mood boards initially to help display your ideas and concepts. You should then begin to develop these ideas through sketches and photographs, and annotate them to explain to your director and cast exactly what will be used in performance. It will be useful for your actors to be provided with rehearsal costumes, particularly if the costumes will be restrictive or affect movement in some way. For example, if you are designing for a period piece, you may wish to provide the females in your cast with 'rehearsal skirts' which mimic the length and style of period dresses. This will help the actors develop their movement in rehearsal so that it is appropriate for the time period.

REHEARSAL AND PRODUCTION

Rehearsal

In the run-up to the performance, you should initially be sketching and developing your costumes. Following this, time will be spent gathering your costumes together and altering, mending, adapting and making them as required. You must also clearly label costumes and create an inventory listing each item, in addition to storing them all appropriately. The following gives some guidance on how you could go about this and the evidence you should create throughout the process.

Preparing a costume plot – A costume plot is basically an organised list of costumes which notes any changes in costume and provides details of all aspects of the costume. Often, we focus on the main outfit and forget about shoes and **accessories**, so it is important to remember all the details. Below is an extract from an example costume plot for *The Importance of Being Earnest* by Oscar Wilde.

ONLINE

Learn more about costume design by following the link at www.brightredbooks.net

NB: In the following table, C refers to clothing, A refers to accessories and F refers to footwear.

Character	Act 1			Act 2			Act 3		
	C	A	F	C	A	F	C	A	F
Lane	Black suit, white shirt	Black bow tie	Black polished shoes						
Algernon	Grey three-piece suit with tailcoat, white shirt and red cravat	Red handkerchief, pocket watch	Black patent slip-on shoes	White three-piece suit with tailcoat	Red handkerchief, pocket watch	White shoes	White three-piece suit with tailcoat	Red handkerchief and bow tie	White shoes
Jack	Grey three-piece suit with tailcoat, white shirt and purple cravat	Purple handkerchief, pocket watch	Black patent slip-on shoes	Black suit and tailcoat, black shirt and tie	Black handkerchief, pocket watch	Black polished shoes	White suit with tailcoat	Purple handkerchief and bow tie	
Gwendolen	Lilac dress	Parasol	Lilac court shoes	Purple day dress	Fan, parasol, white lace gloves	Purple court shoes	Purple day dress	Fan, parasol, white lace gloves	

Technical costume drawings – To construct a costume drawing, you first need to be able to draw a human figure. The easiest and most effective way to do this is by using a geometric approach – this means that the parts of each figure you draw will be proportionate. You can find stencils online to help you do this – simply trace your figure and construct your design on top of it. However, it may be difficult to find exactly what you need and you may prefer to create your own template, which can be adapted to fulfil the body type of the actors/characters.

THINGS TO DO AND THINK ABOUT

Have a go at making an initial costume plot for your extract. Be sure to include any details given in the text and any which you have interpreted.

ONLINE TEST

To test yourself on costume design, head to www.brightredbooks.net

DESIGN — COSTUME 2

INTERACTING WITH YOUR ACTORS

Measuring your actors

There are a number of measurements you will need to take in order to create your made costume and adapt others. When measuring your actors, be sensitive to their needs and find a quiet place to conduct the measuring: it may be upsetting for an actor if his or her waist measurement is announced across a busy drama studio. You must put them at ease and ensure that, when taking the measurements, you quietly note them down and share them discreetly with the actor if they request it. When measuring people you don't know well, or who are of the opposite gender, you may prefer to have someone else to assist, or just to be present as you conduct your measurements.

Once you have taken your measurements, ensure you keep a clear record of them. You may wish to lay these out as an annotated drawing or simple table. Make sure it is clear as you will use it for reference throughout the process of creating your costumes.

ONLINE

There are a number of online guides and tutorials available to help you conduct your measurements. Two you may find useful are at www.brightredbooks.net

Dress/shirt measurement chart

1. Neck _____
2. Over bust _____
3. Bust _____
4. Under bust _____
5. Waist _____
6. Hips _____
7. Neck to heel _____
8. Neck to above knee _____
9. Above knee to ankle _____
10. Arm length _____
11. Shoulder seam _____
12. Arm hole _____
13. Bicep _____
14. Forearm _____
15. Wrist _____
16. V neck cut _____
17. Shoulder to waist _____
18. Waist to above knee _____

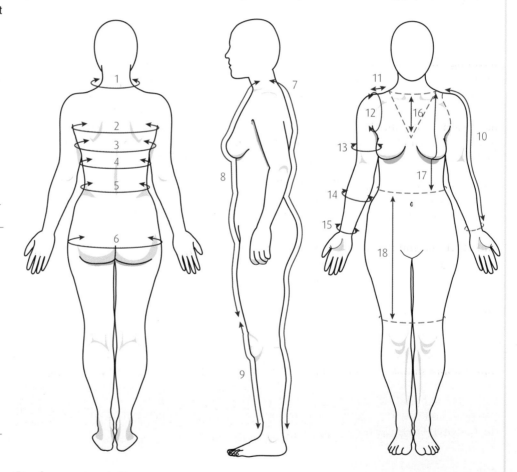

Storing your costumes

It is essential that you store your costumes appropriately, to avoid them being damaged before the performance and to make sure they can all be found by the actors easily. If possible, you should have a dedicated area for this, such as a clothes rail. Label each hanger with the character's name and scene/page reference, and cross-reference this with your costume plot. Hang the clothes on the hanger and place shoes and accessories in a box or bag which is also clearly labelled. You must ensure that all costumes are returned to their appropriate place after being used. In addition, between rehearsals, you may have to clean and mend costumes, so you must have a plan in place for this.

ADAPTING AND MAKING YOUR COSTUMES

You will have to adapt and make costumes as part of the unit and final assessment. This is the most challenging part of the discipline, as well as being the most creative and enjoyable. Below are some ideas on how to adapt and make your costumes.

Adapted costume

You may need to alter a sourced costume to make it fit the actor. As a temporary measure, you may simply need to 'pin' the item – gently folding and using safety pins to secure the fabric. Alternatively, you may wish to permanently alter the garment, which requires more technical skill. Seeking guidance from staff in your school or college (for example, Drama, Art, HE departments) or from a friend or relative may be a good idea, or you can find tutorials online to help. It may be that the garment fits but needs to be changed or added to in some way, for example, by adding embellishments such as feathers, ribbons or buttons, or by altering the colour using dyes or fabric paints. If you choose to change the fabric's colour, ensure you follow the instructions exactly to avoid ruining the item!

The made costume

This can be challenging. If you are a keen sewer or dressmaker, you may find this less daunting. However, if you don't have these skills there are still options for you. Costume includes masks, hats and accessories, so choosing one of these options may be better if you lack the skills needed for making clothing from scratch. Whichever option you choose to create, you must make detailed designs and use the measurements taken from your actor to estimate what materials you need. You should always 'round up' when estimating, as this will ensure you don't run out due to minor mishaps. It is always advisable either to make a pattern or to use an existing one, whatever you are planning to make.

Costume design is a very creative and technical role. It is a good option for an individual who has some experience in the area, but it can also suit someone who wants to learn new skills. It requires an imaginative and hard-working individual who has a clear vision of what they wish to create. It is essential that you work closely with the director, actors and other designers to achieve a shared vision for the production. You must look after all the costumes well between rehearsals and performances in order to maintain them and ensure they are effective in the final performance.

 **DON'T FORGET**

Even if you don't have sewing skills, there are options for making costume.

 THINGS TO DO AND THINK ABOUT

Who is the costume for? The costumes you create and source have to reflect not only the location and setting of the play but also the character being portrayed. Read the extract or section of the text you are planning to design for and note down different elements of the character. Following this, list textures, materials and colours that may personify these attributes. Refer back to these notes throughout your design process as they will remind you of what you initially set out to achieve for the character.

 ONLINE TEST

To test yourself on costume design, head to www.brightredbooks.net

DESIGN — MAKE-UP AND HAIR

Although theatre make-up and hair share similarities with cosmetic make-up and hair, it is essential to note that theatre make-up holds a number of challenges. It does not have to be over-the-top, but it can be, and it must work alongside the chosen theatre lighting and costume design. Therefore, once again, communication and collaboration are crucial to this role. You need to have a steady hand, creative flair, a knowledge of the products you will require and an awareness of the health and safety implications of the role. As with any other production role, there are a number of possible tasks you could carry out in order to be successful.

PRE-PRODUCTION

As with other design areas, research must be carried out initially. You must research the context of the play and undertake more in-depth research and analysis of each character's personality and background in order to adequately design for them and transform every actor into the person they are going to portray. The first decision any make-up designer must make is whether the overall design is going to be **naturalistic** make-up, character make-up or abstract make-up. This decision must be made in conjunction with the director, actors and any other designers involved in the production, as the overall design must be coherent or else it will be distracting for the audience.

Naturalistic design

This should enhance the actor's face and be **realistic**. It may involve some simple **highlighting** and shadowing to intensify features, adding light ageing effects or colour to make the actor appear to be from a specific time period. It can also be used to highlight aspects of the character's personality, for example, red lipstick or specific eye colours or blusher.

Character make-up

If an actor is playing a character considerably older or younger than they are, you may wish to use heavier and more detailed make-up to suggest this. You may need to think about the make-up appropriate for an actor who is playing a character of a specific social status, or you may need to use prosthetics or special effect make-up such as **scarring** or bruising.

Abstract make-up

If the performance has a more stylised form, or if make-up is to be used to help communicate a **central metaphor** or motif, you may wish to design make-up that is more thematic and abstract.

Whichever overall design concept you choose, it is important that there is some justification and reasoning behind it. This should be documented throughout the design process through logbooks, design sketches and make-up plots. Your choice of hair design should also complement the make-up choices you make.

REHEARSAL AND PRODUCTION

Rehearsal

During the rehearsal process you should meticulously plan your make-up design and carry out trials with your actors. The schedule for this should be discussed and planned with your director and actors in advance to ensure you have a fair share of the allotted time.

Design sketches – You can either use a template for a basic face or sketch each one from scratch depending on your abilities and preferences. Your initial sketches should be as detailed as possible and annotated to further describe your thoughts and ideas, linking these to your research.

Make-up plots – Make-up plots are basically diagrams which show the materials you will use and have clear instructions through annotations on how the make-up should be applied to achieve the desired effects. It is advisable to use a template for this, which you can copy or print out a number of times, and you should have a designated plot for each character.

Photo story – If the make-up is very complex, you may wish to take photographs of each stage, or get someone to film you applying the make-up during rehearsal. This is an excellent tool to help you prepare for the performance and ensure you apply the make-up in exactly the same way each time.

Health and safety checks – All make-up contains a variety of ingredients which may cause mild or major allergic reactions in certain people. Most theatre make-up is water-based or grease-based and it is important to carry out a 'patch test' on your actors before you carry out a full practice make-up. A patch test is when you apply a small amount of make-up to a part of an actor's body: the inner forearm or back of the neck (if they have long hair to hide it) are ideal places. Ask your actor to leave the make-up on for an hour or two before washing it off using water only (which avoids any reactions to soap etc. which could confuse the results of your test). After 24–48 hours, if there has been no adverse skin reaction you are safe to carry out your full make-up trial. You should also carry out a patch test if you are planning to use any temporary hair mascaras or sprays to achieve a particular style.

Check the ingredients of all the make-up you are planning to use. Some special effects putties include peanut oil and a number of creams contain caffeine. People can have serious reactions to both of these, so it is important to check, not only with the actors having the make-up applied but also with others in the room, that they don't have an allergy to them, as some people can have reactions without actually coming into direct contact with the substance.

THINGS TO DO AND THINK ABOUT

Discuss the characters involved in the play you are designing for with the director and the actors first. They may have ideas about a character's personality or portrayal which you haven't yet considered but may well be useful to your design concept.

ONLINE

Make-up and hair demonstrations are very popular on the internet. If you have a specific historical era or effect you wish to create, try searching for it online to give yourself a good idea of how to go about achieving it.

DON'T FORGET

Once you have designed your make-up on paper you must complete a make-up trial in good time before the performance. You must also ensure you check the ingredients of the make-up before applying, and check with your subject, in order to avoid allergic reactions.

ONLINE TEST

Test yourself on make-up and hair online at www.brightredbooks.net

DESIGN — LIGHTING

Lighting can greatly enhance a theatrical performance; it can communicate the setting, themes, mood and atmosphere to the audience, and focuses the audience's attention on the action. A badly designed lighting concept can also ruin a production. There is a great deal of collaborative work needed in order for your lighting concepts to be successful – you must liaise with the director, actors and other designers to reach the desired vision for the production.

REHEARSAL AND PERFORMANCE

Pre-production

As with any production role, reading the text and conducting your research are your initial tasks. Following this, you should focus on the extract or act you are working on, listing moods and atmospheres, entrances and exits and any areas of focus. You can then use mood boards, detailed mind-maps or sketches to help communicate your ideas to the cast and director. At this stage, it is important that you are aware of any set pieces or blocking ideas so that you have these in mind as you develop your lighting concepts. There are a number of ways to develop your ideas and document them. Some of these are outlined below.

Assessing equipment – Not all drama studios have the same equipment. And lighting as a specialism is very much constrained by the equipment available to you. More than other aspects of design, lighting is incredibly expensive and there are huge health and safety implications and limitations to its use. These issues must be weighed up and considered, as there are specific SQA guidelines as to how many lanterns you should have access to and how many lighting states you should be able to carry out. Therefore, after you have had some initial ideas about the effects you wish to create, you need to assess what equipment you have at your disposal and how much access you have to it. You could ask yourself the following questions to help you plan how to achieve and/or adapt your concepts to correlate with the resources available.

- What equipment do I need to achieve the effect I want?
- How many lanterns do I have?
- How many of these can I patch?
- How many of these can I focus?
- How many of these are **fresnels**?
- How many are profiles?
- How many **Parcans**?

- How many **floods** do I have?
- Do I have **specials**, for example, **blacklight** or **strobes**?
- Can I change the gels?
- Do I need help to get access to the rig?
- Who can help me with this and how do I arrange this?
- What safety implications do I need to address?

contd

DON'T FORGET

The blocking of the play may change throughout rehearsal, and so your lighting ideas and concepts must be adaptable. You must also make the director aware if there are any fixed points in the lighting rig which cannot be moved so that the action requiring these effects can be blocked in the appropriate area of the stage.

Lighting plot – A lighting plot is a diagram which shows the positions of the lanterns and the areas of the stage or acting areas they highlight. You should use the appropriate symbols for each lantern. It is advisable that you create a 'master' copy of the plot and then use tracing paper or acetate overlays for each scene or section of lighting change. This plot is open to change and should develop throughout the rehearsal process. The lighting plot will allow you to hypothesise how your concepts will look prior to testing them out and will assist you in planning your plugging, patching and focusing of lanterns.

Patching – The lighting board and the lighting rig are usually connected via a panel of plugs and sockets. The process of organising these plugs and sockets into your preferred order is called patching. For example, if you always use two or three lights together to create a '**wash**', you may wish to patch them together so that they come on together using one dimmer or slider on the lighting board. Patching your lights sensibly will make the operation of the lighting board much simpler during performance. You may need to return the wall panel back to its original state after the performance: it is therefore a good idea to photograph or draw a diagram of the original state so that you can do this easily.

Focusing – In order to focus your lights, you will need a quiet performance area, free from actors etc. to ensure safety, and a small team of helpers: someone to operate the board, someone to walk the acting area, and someone to handle the lanterns. It may be that you need to climb ladders to access the lighting rig; if this is the case, you will also need a 'spotter' to steady the ladder. Focusing is the process of moving and fixing lanterns, changing gels and altering **barn doors** to ensure your planned concepts are realised. You may also mark the stage using tape to help the actors stand in the appropriate position in order to be fully lit and seen by the audience.

Lighting cue sheet – A cue sheet should detail all the required cues and levels of each of your chosen lighting states. It should be clear and easy to follow so that you are able to see it and operate the lighting board in low light.

Health and safety – When working as a lighting designer/technician, you must always have your own and others' safety at the forefront of your mind. There are a multitude of areas which could be potentially dangerous. It is essential that you are aware of any dangers and make a clear plan of how to ensure the safety of all involved.

ONLINE

To find out more about theatre lighting, follow the links at www.brightredbooks.net

THINGS TO DO AND THINK ABOUT

List, list, list!

As with any area of theatre production, listing is an effective tool in planning. One of the most important issues for a lighting designer is ensuring safety. Before you do anything else, make a list of potential hazards you may encounter. Once you have listed all possible issues or problems, make a corresponding list which details how you will avoid both injuring yourself and other people. This is called a risk assessment.

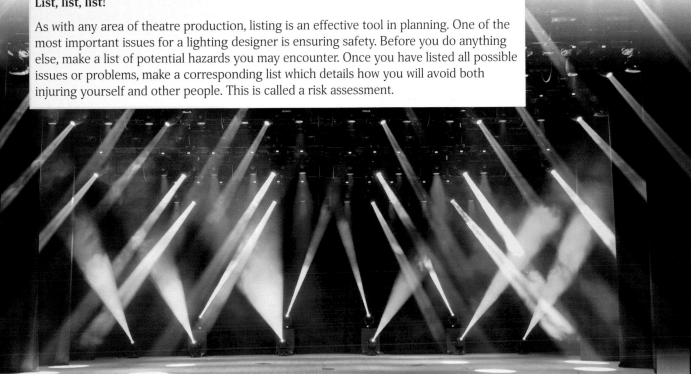

DESIGN — SOUND

Sound can be seen as a soft option by some, as modern technology has made it so much easier to edit, mix and adapt recorded sound. However, what may look like a fairly straightforward production role is actually quite complex, and trickier to demonstrate on paper than the more visually design-based roles. Sound can provide vitally important effects for a production, in addition to creating mood, atmosphere and tension and communicating the setting with the audience. As with lighting and other production roles, there is a great deal of collaborative work needed for your sound concepts to be successful, and you must liaise with the director, actors and other designers to reach the desired vision for the production.

REHEARSAL

Pre-production

As with any production role, reading the text and conducting your research are your initial tasks. Following this, you should focus on the extract or act you are working on, listing moods and atmospheres, entrances and exits and any specific sound requirements in the **stage directions**. You can then use mood boards, detailed mind-maps or sketches to help communicate your sound effect and music ideas to the cast and director. At this stage, it is important that you are aware of any set pieces or blocking ideas, so that you have these in mind as you develop your sound concepts. There are a number of ways to develop your ideas and document them. Some of these are outlined below.

To figure things out, ask yourself the following questions:

- Do I already have the music/sound effect on a device?
- Could I source the effect/music easily online?
- Do I need to use multiple devices?
- Do I have access to the use of a sound mixing desk?
- Can I adapt/cut the sound to fit?
- Do I need to change the positions of speakers to gain the effect?
- Could the effect be created live?
- Could I record the effect to get the appropriate sound?
- Do I need to use microphones?
- Does the sound fit in with the director's and other designers' vision?
- Can I alter the **volume**, base or **pitch** of the sound?
- Are there any safety implications?

On considering these questions, you should record your responses by making notes, creating checklists, mind-maps, posters, etc.

contd

Assessing equipment – As with lighting, sound production is constrained by the resources available to you. Many school theatres and drama studios are fitted with some sort of sound equipment, PA system and mixing desk. If these aren't available to you, however, there is no reason why you can't be imaginative in your sound design and still achieve some interesting sound concepts. After you have come up with your initial concepts, you need to assess the availability of suitable equipment to achieve them, or possibly alter your plans to fit with what is actually available.

Editing sound – In the past, this was quite tricky and involved cutting tapes and splicing them back together. Today, there are a number of ways of doing this using a computer, iPad or other tablet device, or even a mobile phone. Through the use of apps and editing programs you can merge music tracks, and shorten and isolate parts of the track. This can be a time-consuming process and you must be patient and take your time to get your edits right, as this will pay dividends in the future.

Preparing live sound – You may want to use live sound in the production. This must be rehearsed like any other aspect. Unlike recorded sounds, the quality of the sound may alter according to the person creating it. It could be altered by their mood or the timing of the action onstage. For this reason, it is important that amplifying equipment, if required, is put in place as early as possible during rehearsals. This ensures that the sound operator (you) is used to all the ways the sound may alter and is prepared to react accordingly, reducing volume or cutting the effect early if needed.

Recording sound – If you choose to record sound prior to performance, for example **voiceovers** or traffic noise, you must first test the equipment you will use to record the sound, as the quality of sound recorded on devices such as mobile phones can vary greatly.

Cue sheet – A sound cue sheet must be clearly laid out with the cue lines or actions, the source of each sound cue, its volume level and length. The cue sheet may develop and change throughout the rehearsal process and you must be flexible when developing your concepts so that your chosen effects fit with the production as a whole.

Back-up – You should always provide a back-up plan for your sound. Do not rely on the use of online sounds and music, as internet connections can fluctuate and alter; you must have some sort of hard copy of all your sound, whether on an MP3 player, laptop or CD. When using technology, there is always the chance that something might not work as you wish it to.

 **DON'T FORGET**

Rehearsals are as much for the production team as the actors and directors. Ensure you attend all rehearsals so that sound can be incorporated into the process as soon as possible.

 VIDEO LINK

Head to www.brightredbooks.net to watch a clip about sound design.

 THINGS TO DO AND THINK ABOUT

Think about what your 'curtain music' might be. This is what the audience hear as they settle down for the performance. It can be used to set the tone of the whole piece, as the music tends to be heard before 'curtain up'. Mind-map a variety of ideas for this and discuss them with the director and cast to gain feedback on what could best achieve your intentions.

 ONLINE TEST

Test your knowledge of sound design at www.brightredbooks.net

WRITING DRAMA ESSAYS

TEXTUAL ANALYSIS — STRUCTURE OF AN ESSAY

Throughout the Higher Drama course you will study a selected text. Through this study, you will develop a knowledge and understanding of the play's historical, political and social context, its themes and issues, and how you would stage this play from the perspective of an actor, director and designer. To demonstrate this knowledge and understanding, you will write a number of essays, similar to those which will feature in the final exam.

ESSAY STRUCTURE

Although each essay is written from one of three points of view (actor, director, designer); they share a common structure. To explain how an essay should be structured and how best to respond to an essay question, in the following pages we will work through some example questions and answers. The first example question we will address is from the perspective of an actor:

'As an actor, give details of **five** ways in which your chosen character creates dramatic tension throughout your selected text.'

DON'T FORGET

You must use textual references from the play to help you to justify your answer.

Explain how, as an actor, you would help build this dramatic tension. (These need to be related to the first part of this question.)

Introductions and conclusions

You do not gain marks for your introduction or conclusion. However, it is important to provide details of how you intend to approach the question in the introduction and sum up how your essay has addressed the question in the conclusion. To address our first example question, the introduction might look something like this:

> **Example:**
>
> In Harold Pinter's 'The Birthday Party', the character of Stanley creates dramatic tension through his interactions with others, his battle for status and his character breakdown. In this essay I will explain how, as an actor, I will portray this through the acting concepts of voice, movement, proxemics and use of props and costume.

In a similar vein, the conclusion might look something like this:

> **Example:**
>
> In conclusion, I have demonstrated how Stanley's need for power and status is his undoing and how this creates dramatic tension throughout 'The Birthday Party' by Harold Pinter. I have also identified how I would use acting concepts in order to heighten and communicate this tension with the audience.

DON'T FORGET

Use the language of the question in your introduction, your conclusion and throughout the essay to keep yourself on track.

The main body of the text

If we look closely at the example question again, it is easy to see how the response could be split into two sections, A and B.

> A: As an **actor**, give details of **five** ways in which your chosen character creates **dramatic tension** throughout your selected text. (You must use textual references from the play to help you to justify your answer.)

contd

Part A asks you to provide five ways in which the character creates dramatic tension. It also asks you to provide textual examples and justify each point you make.

> B: Explain how, as an **actor**, you would help **build** this **dramatic tension**.
> (These need to be related to the first part of this question.)

Part B asks you to explain how you would build the tension through your acting concepts. It also asks you to relate this back to Part A of the question.

There are two ways to approach this. One way is to use an all A/all B structure, answering all of Part A and then all of the B points. Although this is a sound way of approaching the textual analysis essay, it also invites repetition, as you need to link the response in Part B back to your Part A point, and it needs to be clear how they are linked. It may also result in you getting confused while writing the essay.

The second possible structure is A/B. When using this structure, you make your detailed A point and immediately follow it with your B point. This structure removes the need for repetition and is more direct in addressing the question.

Whichever structure you choose to adopt, it is important that within the A part of the essay you use the PRD rule:

- Make a POINT
- Give a textual REFERENCE
- Provide DEPTH in your analysis

According to the SQA marking guidance, the first A mark (A✓) is awarded for making the point and providing the textual reference (P and R). The second A mark (A1) is awarded for the depth of analysis (D).

Example:

> P: In the final scene of 'The House of Bernarda Alba' by Federico García Lorca, Adela builds dramatic tension throughout her exchange with her elder sister Martirio. Adela creates **dramatic irony** as Martirio wasn't aware that Adela knew she also had feelings for Pepe el Romano, who is engaged to be married to their other sister, Angustias.
>
> R: 'How you'd love to be there yourself.' (A✓)
>
> D: The revelations and realisations in this scene are important in highlighting the issues of the play and the girls' need to be free from their mother's tyrannous reign. Adela shows that she is not innocent and willing to stand up to others, including her mother. This reflects Lorca's own life and his inability to be himself and escape the social stigma which led to his death. (A1)

VIDEO LINK

To be or not to be ... Watch David Tennant's performance of the Hamlet soliloquy at www.brightredbooks.net and note how the lone actor, without any interaction, creates dramatic tension through silence, pause, eye contact and vocal delivery.

ONLINE TEST

To test yourself on structuring your essay, head to www.brightredbooks.net

THINGS TO DO AND THINK ABOUT

Is there a character in your selected text who creates dramatic tension? Make a list of the ways in which the character does this throughout the play. In addition to this, you could cross-reference with useful quotes that highlight how tension is created.

WRITING DRAMA ESSAYS

PART A

In Part A of the essay, you are required to demonstrate your knowledge and understanding of your selected text. Whether you are answering as an actor, director or designer, the first part of the essay is, in essence, the same. You could be asked about a variety of areas from your selected text and you should do plenty of practice in the run-up to the exam so that there are no surprises.

PART A AREAS

In an essay, you could be asked to discuss the opening scene, a key scene, the final scene or the whole play – which isn't always specifically stated in the question, but if none of the other options are mentioned it is implied that you should discuss the play in its entirety.

You will always be asked to make five points related to a given area. These areas could be:

- **Audience response** – How the audience **reacts**.
- **Emotional responses** – How a character or audience reacts to a given situation.
- **Character relationships** – How they are, change and alter.
- **Mood and atmosphere** – The emotions created by the action of the play.
- **Dramatic tension** – The driving force of the play and how it is created.
- **The play's genre** – The overall style of the drama.
- **Dramatic features** – Events of the play, its style, design or performance issues.
- **Changes in status** – Power relationships of the characters.
- **Changes in circumstance** – How aspects of the plot/action affect individual characters.
- **Key features** – Important performance, plot or design aspects.
- **Key moments** – Important events that alter the course of the play.
- **Character feelings** – How they feel towards others.
- **Character motivation** – What drives the character, what they hope to achieve.
- **Character personality** – What the character is like.
- **Themes and issues** – What the play is about, recurring motifs, the playwright's context.
- **Conflict** – Between characters/due to the play's events.

Example:

DON'T FORGET

You must use textual exemplification to help justify any points you make in Part A. The easiest way to do this is to quote accurately.

The Prime of Miss Jean Brodie

1. As a director, describe how you would like your audience to react to **five** key moments in your selected text. You should use textual references to support your answer.

In Act 1 of 'The Prime of Miss Jean Brodie', a key moment is her initial speech – 'Little girls, I am in the business of putting old heads on young shoulders and all of my girls are the crème de la crème.' In this speech she outlines her manifesto for what she sees as her 'vocation'. However, it is immediately clear to the audience that it is her own ego which she is concerned with rather than her pupils' wellbeing, as she immediately digresses into talking about herself and her past experiences. This is a key moment as the audience is fully aware from the outset that the play is not going to be about a 'normal' teacher or school.

contd

ONLINE

Check out the SQA
Specimen Question
Paper for more examples at
www.brightredbooks.net

Example:

2. As an actor, describe **five** ways in which a central character highlights the themes and issues of your selected text. You must use detailed textual references to support your answer.

In 'Lovers' by Brian Friel, Mag highlights the theme of religion. Throughout the play she makes references to religious figures and how she feels about them.

'Sister Pascal says you will search the lists of the canonized, but you will search in vain for a Saint that smoked ...'

This highlights that Mag is rebelling against her religious teachings (by smoking) but still retains them and is heavily influenced by them. In the 1960s in Ireland it was very difficult for an unmarried mother as she would be sent to a Magdalene laundry or forced to go to England for an abortion – as it was against the law in Ireland. In the case of Mag and Joe 'doing the right thing' and getting married, it is very clear how heavily religion features in their lives and here, in the above quote, it is also clear that Mag is, in a small way, rebelling against it.

Example:

3. As a designer, explain **five** ways in which a key scene creates dramatic tension in your selected text. You should use detailed textual references to justify your answer.

In 'A Taste of Honey' by Shelagh Delaney, Act 2, Scene 1 is key as it builds to the climax of the play. At the very beginning of the scene we meet Geof and Jo in a darkened room. This instantly begins to create tension, as immediately prior to this we have heard Jo and the boy having lots of fun at the fair:

'Jo and a boy can be heard playing together. When they enter the flat they have been playing about with a bunch of brightly coloured balloons. It is summer now and Jo's pregnancy is quite obvious.'

The juxtaposition of the playful opening to the scene and its immediate change to Jo 'as she falls on a couch in a darkened room' initiates tension, as Jo has been enjoying herself but the change in light signifies her exhaustion, and the fact that she is accompanied by Geof and not the boy also suggests that everything is not as it first seemed.

A Taste of Honey

 THINGS TO DO AND THINK ABOUT

What are the similarities between the examples above? Now that you know the 'ingredients' for a Part A response, write a few paragraphs for your own selected text. You may wish to use the SQA's exemplar paper to practise responding to actual exam questions.

ONLINE TEST

Take the 'Part A' test at
www.brightredbooks.net

PART B — DIRECTING

Part B is closely linked to Part A. It is here that you respond as a director, actor or designer. In the following section, we will look at how to structure a response from the perspective of a director. Some of the advice here will also apply to Part B from the actor's and designer's point of view.

DIRECTING

As discussed in the previous pages, although the way you are asked to discuss the question and the areas to be addressed will vary, the way to approach them is the same. It is important to note that you should have a clear idea of how you will direct your production, and you can apply this to whichever question is posed.

ASPECTS OF DIRECTING

The most important aspect of your direction is how it communicates with the audience and the impact it would have. You may be asked to describe how your direction would work in performance or how you would direct your actors in rehearsal. In either case, you must focus on how you will communicate the aspects discussed in Part A through your directorial concepts. Possible areas to discuss and describe may include the following:

- **Pre-show** – What the audience experiences before the play officially starts. For example, the cast could be interacting onstage or with the audience, or you may choose to play particular music or project something onstage which suggests the required mood and atmosphere.

- **Stage proxemics** – The placing of your characters onstage and how this shows their relationship. For example, you could place your actors close to one another to show they are in a close relationship.

- **Positioning** – This is developed during the blocking phase of directing and involves positioning characters, props and set onstage to communicate meaning to the audience. For example, you could position a character centre-stage to convey that the character is the **protagonist**, so that the audience focuses on them.

- **Use of levels** – Similar to positioning and often used to convey status.

- **Characterisation** – How the director leads the actors through developing the character so that they can convey this to the audience. For example, you could use hot seating in rehearsal to give your actors a deep understanding of their character's history.

- **Character interaction** – How you will direct your actors to react and interact with each other to demonstrate their relationships.

- **Acting style** –If you are discussing a particular style of play, such as melodrama, the acting used in the performance should portray this.

- **Voice and movement** – How you will direct your actors to use these in order to communicate meaning.

- **Actor/audience relationship** – This can be established through a character addressing the audience directly, using **asides** or through **eye contact**. It is about creating an emotional response in the audience so that it shares the desired response to a particular character or situation.

- **Special effects** – Pyrotechnics, smoke machines, etc.

- **Production areas** – Lighting, sound, props, set design, costume, make-up and hair.

- **Drama media** – Projections, video footage, soundscapes, etc.

DON'T FORGET

If you are asked about rehearsal/workshops, you should discuss rehearsal techniques: for example, character profiles/cards, character iceberg, character maps, 'role on the wall', role play, writing in role, hot seating, thought tunnel, thought tracking, visualisation, tableau, role reversal, improvisation, use of prop, use of costume.

DON'T FORGET

Directing concepts are your ideas and how you would put them into action. They must be closely linked to the points you have made in Part A of the essay.

contd

Example:

You will recognise the first part of this question from page 60. The first example given below is the 'in performance' style; the second is an 'in rehearsal' type question.

1 As a director, describe how you would like your audience to react to **five** key moments in your selected text. You should use textual references to support your answer.

Explain how you would use **five** directing concepts to achieve your desired audience response in performance. (These must be linked to the first part of the question.) (B1)

The first directing concept I would use to highlight the key moment above is proxemics. I would have the girls positioned around Betty's bed USR and Abigail centre-stage. This would highlight that she is the focus during her speech and show the distance between her and the other girls, and it would elevate her status as she is exercising power over them. When she gets to 'pointy reckoning', I would have her move towards the girls slowly and speak in a cold, calm tone. Abi would then turn away from the girls and speak out towards the audience, again showing she is powerful as she doesn't even need to make eye contact with them, yet they react fearfully. This would help create the shocked reaction in the audience as it further conveys how dark a character she is and how she holds power over the girls and that all the things she denied to Parris earlier are actually true.

Explain how you would use **five** rehearsal techniques that would help achieve your desired audience response in performance. (These must be linked to the first part of the question.) (B.2)

The first rehearsal technique I would use would be improvisation. I would get the actors playing Abigail, Mary, Betty and the other girls to improvise a scene where they are teenage girls in the present day sneaking out to go to an all-night party. This would help the actors connect with their characters as they could draw on their own experiences and the excitement they felt in their own lives when doing something that is not allowed. During the improvisation, I would tell them other information at certain points to establish that the actor playing Abi is the ringleader and gives the others drugs, which 'Betty' takes a reaction to. They would then move on to improvise a scene where they are going to be questioned by the police and 'Abi' is telling them to keep quiet. This would help the actors to understand the feelings of their characters, which in turn will allow them to communicate this onstage. It will add to the shock the audience feels, as the actors will give a very realistic portrayal of the emotions they experienced during the improvisation, and the genuine fear they have will be palpable and so felt by the audience.

ONLINE

Follow the link to the exemplar paper at www.brightredbooks.net

 THINGS TO DO AND THINK ABOUT

Read the example response to Part A on page 60 directly before the two Part B examples above. Consider how they complement each other and apply this to your own essay writing.

ONLINE TEST

Test yourself on Part B at www.brightredbooks.net

PART B — ACTING AND DESIGNING

AS AN ACTOR

As with the director questions, as an actor you will be asked to explain or describe your chosen performance concepts or acting concepts and how they will be used to communicate meaning to the audience. It is also possible that you could be asked to explain how you would prepare for a role and communicate the desired impact on the audience. The areas you will discuss are similar to those previously detailed in the director section, but the perspective is on how you as the actor will communicate with your audience through your performance.

Acting concepts

Acting concepts include characterisation, acting techniques, acting style, voice, movement, proxemics, interaction between characters, use of costume, use of prop, and use of make-up and hair.

Note: For rehearsal techniques see the section on directing (page 17).

Example:

The first part of the question is recognisable from page 61.

DON'T FORGET

Directing and acting questions are very similar, so you must be careful how you word your response.

As an actor, describe **five** ways in which a central character highlights the themes and issues of your selected text. You must use detailed textual references to support your answer.

Describe in detail how, as an actor, you would use **five** acting concepts to highlight the themes and issues to the audience. (These must be clearly related to the first part of the question.)

To highlight the religious theme when portraying Mag, I would use movement and positioning. I would stand centre-stage and mime out crossing myself before standing with my hands clasped in prayer, mimicking Sister Pascal. I will also roll my eyes to portray that I do not agree with the nun's views, highlighting the rebellion Mag has towards religion. After poking fun at Sister Pascal, I will glance towards the sky, demonstrating that she is checking if God is watching. This would highlight the theme of religion and rebellion, as Mag is the focus at this point and the audience will be drawn to her positioning. Also, through my movement it will be really obvious that although Mag is rebelling against her religion it is in fairly small ways, as she still abides by its customs in a general sense.

AS A DESIGNER

As with directing and acting, it is required in the design essay that you discuss five different design concepts. These can be taken from any production area. However, you will lose credit if you fail to cover a variety of different areas.

Design concepts

- **Venue** – Building or location where the performance is being staged.
- **Period** – The historical time period and location of the play.
- **Shifts in time** – If the time period of the play changes through **flashbacks/flash forwards**.
- **Stage configuration** – How the performance space is set up – proscenium arch, traverse, inverted traverse, promenade, thrust, in the round.
- **Actor–audience relationship.**
- **Immediate circumstances** – What are the immediate requirements of the action? For example, if a stage direction states that the character sits at a table, the designer would have to source or create the appropriate table and chair.
- **Onstage/offstage world** – What we see onstage and how this continues offstage. For example, if a character exits to an unseen room, this would be the offstage world of the play.
- **Set design, props, costume, make-up, lighting, sound, drama media.**
- **Fabric and materials.**
- **Colour and style.**
- **Age, personality, status and relationships of the characters.**

Example:

You will recognise the first part of this question from page 61.

1. As a designer, explain **five** ways in which a key scene creates dramatic tension in your selected text. You should use detailed textual references to justify your answer.

(b) Explain how you would use **five** design concepts in order to create dramatic tension in this scene. (These need to be linked to the first part of the question.)

Initially, I would use a UV light which would highlight two large fluorescent balloons, one pink and one blue, as they float towards the roof – these would not be real balloons but would be lowered via the flies and would be on wires, so the floating to the ceiling would be slow and gradual as the voices of Jo and the boy are heard offstage. The remainder of the stage would be in blackout. Following the balloons' disappearance, I would use a blue/grey gel on a single fresnel to create a gloomy and tense atmosphere. This lantern would be focused on the sofa centre-stage. As the dialogue begins, I would fade in a low grey/blue wash so that the actors can be seen and heard. The use of this cold lighting state would create tension, as we have just heard a happy exchange offstage and the balloons floating by gave the audience hope that Jo's fortunes were changing. The scene they are then faced with negates this and creates tension as a result.

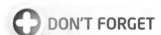 **DON'T FORGET**

You may favour a particular area in your practical work, but that doesn't mean you will write your best essays in that particular area!

 VIDEO LINK

Learn more about design concepts by watching the clip at www.brightredbooks.net

 ONLINE TEST

Head to www.brightredbooks.net for a test on Part B.

 THINGS TO DO AND THINK ABOUT

There are pros and cons to each essay type. It is important that you practise each type of essay, as you don't know which one will suit you best in the final exam. Have a look at the example essays on the SQA website and try out a variety of director/designer/actor essays so that you are adept at writing each type.

PERFORMANCE ANALYSIS ESSAY

Throughout the Higher Drama course, in addition to analysing a theatrical text, you will also be required to analyse theatrical performances. This will ultimately be assessed in the form of an essay in Section Two of the written exam paper.

Kill Johnny Glendenning by DC Jackson, a co-production between the Royal Lyceum Theatre Edinburgh and Citizens Theatre

WHY ANALYSE PERFORMANCE?

Analysing a theatrical performance is not an easy task. However, it is an invaluable part of the course, as you will develop your understanding of drama and theatre not only as an audience member but also as a creative performer yourself. Theatre can inspire you, in terms of ideas for both the Drama and Production Skills units, in addition to allowing you to develop and gain a lifelong critical eye. No longer will you simply enjoy or dislike a piece of theatre, but you will be able to articulate exactly what appealed to you and why.

What should you see?

There is a myriad of theatre out there and it is advisable that you see as much as possible. You can write about a wide variety of theatrical genres, but you are not permitted to analyse a **musical**, ballet or opera; although these are all performed in theatres, they do not necessarily involve dialogue and are disciplines in their own right. You can watch live professional theatre performances or **amateur** performances – providing they are of a high standard and use a variety of production concepts and theatrical media. You can also watch a recorded theatre performance, providing it was presented within **the past two years**. Your drama teacher will probably arrange for you to attend the theatre as a class or let you view a recorded performance in class. However, you can still view other productions on your own initiative, and it is a good idea to consume as much theatre as possible.

The theatre can be expensive, but there are ways to keep the costs down. Many theatres hold preview performances where the ticket prices are heavily discounted. Some theatres also provide reduced rates for students, or you can watch recorded theatre performances online or, occasionally, on BBC Four.

contd

ONLINE

Digital Theatre online has a library of theatrical performances from a variety of theatre companies, including the Young Vic, the National Theatre and the Royal Shakespeare Company. Performances can be streamed on a pay-per-view basis or downloaded for unlimited viewing. Follow the link at www.brightredbooks.net

Before the performance

After deciding on what production to see, there is some background work to be done to prepare for the performance. You can visit the producing company's website: most companies have information online about their past productions, ethos, message or intentions, and upcoming productions. They also often provide education packs and trailers for their upcoming productions. By looking at these and taking notes on the company, you can give yourself a clear idea of what to expect from the performance and the work of the theatre company.

During the performance

During the performance, some people like to take notes on what is happening onstage. However, this isn't always the best idea as you might miss important action. It may be better to enjoy the performance as it happens and jot down a few brief notes during the interval and on the way home. You can also revisit photographs, trailers and other information online to remind you about the performance afterwards, and you can discuss it with your peers or family as they may have noticed aspects that you hadn't picked up on.

 **DON'T FORGET**

Enjoy the performance for what it is and discuss and take notes afterwards.

Organising your thoughts

Through discussing with others who shared your performance experience, and through your initial research and the observations you noted about the performance, you will have a wealth of information, and it may be a little daunting to work out exactly how to form that into an essay. You may find mind-mapping useful at this stage in order to organise your thoughts. Initially, it would be helpful to break down your thoughts into the separate production areas and simply list what production concepts were employed in the performance.

Example:

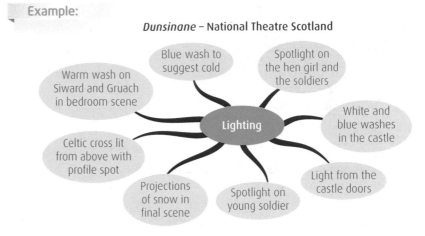

Dunsinane – National Theatre Scotland

Warm wash on Siward and Gruach in bedroom scene

Blue wash to suggest cold

Spotlight on the hen girl and the soldiers

Celtic cross lit from above with profile spot

Lighting

White and blue washes in the castle

Projections of snow in final scene

Spotlight on young soldier

Light from the castle doors

Following your initial mind-maps, it may then be useful to write some more detailed examples and notes examining what the production areas communicated to you as the audience and how effective they were.

Example:

The spotlight on the young soldier, as he delivered his monologues on the apron of the stage, highlighted the isolation he felt and provided the audience with a clear focus during these sections of the performance. The change in colour from a warm orange tone to a much colder blue/white towards the end of the play showed how he had become less hopeful and naive, and much more hardened through fighting in the invasion and being far away from home. The use of lighting highlighted the tone of the soldier's letters home to his mother.

 THINGS TO DO AND THINK ABOUT

Have a look at the National Theatre of Scotland's website http://www.nationaltheatrescotland.com/

Choose a production from the upcoming season which is accessible to you. Take down some notes from the website and check if there are resources which are of use to you. This should give you a strong idea of exactly what information is available to you before, and following, your visit to the theatre.

 ONLINE

Head to www.brightredbooks.net and test yourself on this topic.

STRUCTURE OF THE ESSAY

Although you cannot predict exactly what will be asked of you in the final exam, there is a specific form and structure for a performance analysis essay. First, the question will have a clear focus: for example, its themes and issues. You will then choose two production areas from a choice of four and explain how these aspects address the focus of the question. You will then be required to analyse the effectiveness of the performance and the impact it had on you – the audience. You must include an introduction and conclusion; although you don't receive marks for these, it is important to include them as they give the person marking the essay a good awareness of the performance you are analysing and how you will approach the essay.

INTRODUCTION

Your introduction must provide an overview of the performance, including the following information:

- The name of the play
- The company which performed the play
- Where and when you saw the production
- The director's name
- The style of the production
- A (very brief) plot synopsis
- Reference to the question
- The production areas you will discuss

Dunsinane – National Theatre of Scotland

Example:

1. Consider the themes and issues of the play in a performance you have seen recently.

   Now select **two** production areas from the list below:
   - ACTING
   - DIRECTOR'S INTENTIONS
   - COSTUME
   - LIGHTING

   In your analysis, identify and explain in detail the ways in which your **two** production areas helped to communicate the themes and issues of the play and enhanced your appreciation of the performance.

Introduction:

Frantic Assembly's production of 'Lovesong' by Abi Morgan follows an elderly man coming to terms with his wife's illness and eventual assisted suicide. Throughout the performance, the action weaves through the couple's lives together and how their relationship has altered and changed over the years. The themes explored through the play are love, relationships, family and old age. These themes were demonstrated clearly through the acting and lighting used in the performance.

CONCLUSION

The conclusion of the essay should sum up your findings and address the different elements of the question.

Example:

2. Think about the social **and/or** political **and/or** historical context of a performance you have seen recently.

   Now select **two** of the following production areas:
   - ACTING
   - SETTING
   - PERFORMANCE SPACE
   - LIGHTING

   In your analysis, identify and explain, in detail, the ways in which your **two** selected performance areas helped communicate the social **and/or** political **and/or** historical context of the play and enhanced your appreciation of the performance.

Conclusion:

To conclude, 'Kill Johnny Glendenning' is a production that clearly illustrates the social, political and historical context through the clever use of acting and setting. The audience's response to the humour of the production and their shock at the more gory aspects showed that the desired dramatic impact was achieved.

contd

MAIN BODY

The main body of the essay should explain how your two chosen production areas contribute to the aspect addressed in the question. The focus of this is always the impact or effect on the audience, as this is the measure of how successful the performance has been. The structure is fairly straightforward. As in a textual analysis essay, it is split into two parts – to avoid confusion we will refer to these as 1 and 2 (production area 1 and production area 2). You can choose either to tackle the essay by addressing all of production area 1 and then all of production area 2, or to alternate between area 1 and area 2. This will be looked at in more detail in the following pages, but an example of each is given below.

Whichever approach you choose to use, it is important that you are consistent. This will prevent you from getting muddled and should ensure that you cover all of the required points and in a suitable amount of detail.

DON'T FORGET

Although they achieve no marks, introductions and conclusions are very helpful for the person marking your essay!

Example:

Question 1 – All 1, all 2 approach

The theme of relationships, and in particular fidelity, was clearly shown in the scene with the young couple, when Maggie explains to her husband that, although tempted, she did not have an affair. Here, Leanne Rowe successfully used movement to portray her shame and also her love for her husband. Maggie stood behind a chair with her hands on the back of it and kept the chair between herself and her husband. She shifted her weight from foot to foot and turned away from her husband at points to show she was uncomfortable. However, when she comes to explain the truth and the fact that 'I love my husband', she fixes eye contact with him and moves past the chair towards him. This communicates clearly that she does love him and wants the marriage to work, and it had a strong impact on the audience as many could empathise with both sides in the situation, which was very complex.

Towards the end of the play, the strength of Billy and Maggie's love for each other is really tested and shown to be very strong. Throughout, there has been conflict between the older version of the couple as Billy tries to come to terms with Maggie's decision to die. This is clearly shown through the actor's use of movement as he physicalises his internal emotions and conflicts through a stylised solo sequence . . .

Example:

Question 2 – alternating 1/2 approach

The social context of stereotyping is depicted in 'Kill Johnny Glendenning' through acting, particularly in the character of Skootch. It is made clear that he is a stereotypically immature character through use of his fast and excitable voice. Skootch seems very keen and excited about his job, being a 'gangster'. For example, Skootch used a very excited tone and loud volume with a high pitch, which made him sound very childlike. The impact on the audience was of entertainment at Skootch's behaviour as they found it very funny, especially when he was swearing as the audience all laughed at this point.

The social context of stereotyping could also be seen through use of setting. The set of Act 1 made it clear to the audience before Auld Jim had even been introduced that the owner of the house was a working-class farmer, as stereotypes are often used in a drama to quickly establish a character. The set of Act 1 shows a very small living space of a kitchen/dining area with a small toilet joined to the side of the room. This lack of living space helps to clarify Auld Jim's lack of wealth, and therefore that he is of the working class. The piles of tyres, the hares and the poorly built house are also demonstrative of a stereotypical farmer of a low income. The audience showed uncomfortable facial expressions, showing that they were not used to seeing such an ill-kept home.

THINGS TO DO AND THINK ABOUT

Look at the examples above and consider which one makes most sense to you. Whichever approach seems more logical to you is probably the best one to use initially. However, this may change as you become more adept at writing this type of essay. Visit the SQA website and have a look at the specimen papers there, then have a go at planning an essay – once you have seen a production, that is!

ONLINE

Follow the link at www.brightredbooks.net to practise a past paper.

ONLINE TEST

Test yourself on this topic at www.brightredbooks.net

QUESTION TYPES — PERFORMANCE ASPECTS

As with textual analysis, you also need to demonstrate your understanding of the play being performed and how your chosen areas of the production demonstrate the aims of the performance. The aspects of the performance that you will be asked to analyse vary, but there is also close crossover between them.

WHAT YOU MAY BE ASKED TO DISCUSS

The following list is taken from SQA support documents and provides an overview of what areas are covered in a performance analysis essay.

Performance analysis will consider areas such as:

- The genre, theme and social, historical and/or theatrical context of the performance

- The company performing the play

- The performance space

- The director's intentions and effectiveness

- The acting and development of characters

- The design concepts and their effectiveness – set, props, costume, make-up, lighting, sound/effects

- Audience **reaction**

- Overall impact

In order to reflect the way these areas have been addressed in questions posed by the SQA so far, and to provide further detail of exactly what each aspect covers, the following more detailed list could be useful in addressing the performance analysis essay:

Contrasts – A theatrical contrast involves elements of the plot/design/context etc. being strikingly different from something else in juxtaposition or close association. For example, you might say that using bright costumes and a black set would be a clear contrast. The contrast could also be between characters, locations, or plot developments – virtually anything that appears in the performance.

Themes – The overall or underlying theme(s) of the play: for example, love, betrayal, war.

Areas – What the play is about. This is very similar to theme and you may use the same examples as you would for a theme question.

Issues – Again, related to theme, but about the smaller aspects of the play. For example, if the theme is love the related issues could be relationship breakdowns, forbidden love, etc.

Ideas – Again, similar to theme. The central idea could be more conceptual and less literal than a theme.

Social/political/religious context – These are related to the background of the play, where and when it is set, and what issues are faced by the characters.

DON'T FORGET

This is not an exhaustive list.

DON'T FORGET

A performance analysis essay could take a variety of forms. You need to work very hard during your general preparation to make the job of actually writing the essay very easy!

contd

Message – What the play is trying to communicate to the audience.

Purpose – Similar to message, but more about the desired effect on the audience: for example, to educate them about an issue, highlight a point of view, or achieve an emotional response (to laugh/cry etc.).

Genre/style – **Comedy**, **tragedy**, physical theatre, **verbatim** theatre, etc.

Director's/company's intentions – What the company or director is trying to communicate through the performance. For example, a production of *Macbeth* set in the present day could be staged to highlight current political issues and tensions caused by elitism.

PREPARING TO TACKLE THE PERFORMANCE ASPECTS

After your initial research into the production, having viewed the performance and prepared your notes and mind-maps, it is time to begin to formulate your thoughts. At this point, you may not know what form the essay question will take, so it is essential to prepare for all the aspects outlined on the previous page and above. It is advisable that you do this before applying it to the production elements (which will be explained in the following pages). This may seem a bit general at this stage, but it will make your job easier as you move forward, as you should be able to find examples from all of the different production concepts to support the notes you create next.

By making detailed responses to the following questions, you should create a robust set of notes that will stand you in good stead later on.

1. What are the main themes and issues addressed in the play?

2. Discuss the plot and how this communicates the play's themes and issues.

3. What is the genre/style of the play?

4. How is this communicated through the action of the play?

5. Discuss the context of the play:
   - Where is it set?
   - When is it set?
   - Is there a political situation reflected in the play?
   - Is there a social issue reflected in the play?
   - Is there a particular historical or cultural background reflected in the play?

6. What is the main purpose of the production?

7. What is the director/theatre company trying to communicate through the production?

8. What contrasts are there in the production?

ONLINE

Although a performance analysis essay is not, strictly speaking, a review of a performance, there are a number of similarities between the two. It may well be useful to have a look at the guide at www.brightredbooks.net for some inspiration!

THINGS TO DO AND THINK ABOUT

Use YouTube!

Often, theatre companies, actors and directors run their own blogs or upload promotional material to YouTube. You may also find interviews from local and national news sites and radio programmes which feature the company/director. Revisiting the company's or theatre's website may also be useful, as more materials are often added during the run of the production. These videos and social media content may well give you an insight into their intentions for the production and provide you with direct opinion and information about the performance you have seen which will help you later when you come to write essays about it.

ONLINE TEST

Test yourself online at www.brightredbooks.net

PERFORMANCE AREAS

As discussed in the previous section, in a performance analysis essay you will be required to analyse an aspect of the performance. You will do this by focusing on two performance areas. These include the production roles – acting, directing, props, costume, lighting, sound, set, make-up and hair – but can also be worded as use of performance space, setting, director's intentions, use of projection and dramatic media.

There is some crossover between the elements listed above. For example, set/setting and use of performance space share similarities, and you would discuss some of the same aspects in each of these. Similarly, dramatic media is closely related to both lighting and sound, as you may discuss projections or explosions within each, for example. For each area, there are a variety of elements you may wish to discuss, and you will need to ensure that the points you make closely relate to the performance aspect required by the question. Below is a list of performance elements and examples of what you may wish to discuss in an essay.

CHOOSING PERFORMANCE AREAS

You will be given a choice of four performance areas. As you don't know which options you will be given to choose from in the final exam, it is essential that you are prepared to answer from as wide a variety of them as possible. The following notes and advice are based on SQA marking schemes and are designed to help you think about what you could discuss in the essay. This is not exhaustive, but based on current marking guidelines.

Acting

- Production concept
- Acting style – naturalistic, stylised, melodramatic, etc.
- Pre-show – what happens before 'curtain up', for example, as the audience enters
- Period – when the performance is set and how the acting reflects this
- Characterisation
- **Multi-role** – one actor playing more than one character
- Voice
- Movement
- Relationship of text and physicality – how physical action reflects the dialogue and action
- Interaction
- **Ensemble** – all the actors working as part of a whole
- Actor–audience relationship – how the actors connect with the audience
- Mood, atmosphere and tension
- Innovation/creativity – is there anything new or particularly creative in the acting approach?

Set

- Production concept
- Time period
- Location(s)
- Central metaphor – an item being used to symbolise something else
- **Visual images**
- Style and **tone** – a link between the elements of the set, for example, all Victorian furniture painted white
- **Illusionistic setting** – use of perspective or positioning to deceive the eye, for example, use of a backdrop that depicts a road going into the distance
- **Stylised setting** – non-naturalistic setting
- Line, mass, composition, texture, colour, hue, saturation
- Use of scenic flats, stage cloths, **backcloths**, cyclorama
- Use of rostra, projections

Lighting

- Overall production concept
- Pre-show
- Period
- Sources – where the light comes from
- Naturalistic LFX (lighting effects) – reflects literally the environment of the action
- Abstract LFX – represents ideas, moods and atmospheres
- The part LFX plays in suggestion
- Expectation/tension
- Changes in mood/atmosphere
- Changes in location
- Environmental LFX – lighting which reflects the environment, for example, orange to suggest firelight
- Special LFX – strobe, UV, follow spot, etc.
- Highlighting action/actors/set/props, etc.

contd

Sound

- Overall production concept
- Pre-show
- Period
- Naturalistic SFX (sound effects), abstract SFX
- Recorded SFX, **live SFX**
- Use of music
- Use of soundscapes
- The part sound plays in suggestion
- Creating/releasing tension
- The onstage/offstage world
- Mood/atmosphere
- Location/environmental SFX
- Special SFX
- Diegetic sound – sound the characters and audience hear
- Non-diegetic sound – sound only the audience hear, for example, mood music

Performance space

- Selection of the performance venue
- Atmosphere of the performance venue
- Pre-show
- Staging choice
- Actor–audience relationship
- Stage positioning
- **Auditorium** configuration and audience position/sight lines
- Impact of set/changes of set
- Visual **imagery**
- Use of digital media

Props

- The overall production concept
- Age
- Personality
- Status/changes in status
- Immediate circumstances
- Time and place
- Context
- Central metaphor
- Visual images

- Materials/fabrics, colour palette, tone and style
- Illusionistic or representative ideas
- How the prop is used
- Style and tone

Costume

- The overall production concept
- Age
- Personality
- Status/changes in status
- Immediate circumstances
- Time and place
- Central metaphor
- Visual images
- Costume fabrics, colour palette, tone and style
- Illusionistic or representative ideas

Make-up and hair

- The overall production concept
- Age
- Personality
- Status/changes in status
- Immediate circumstances
- Time and place
- Central metaphor
- Visual images
- Choice of make-up, colour palette, tone and style
- Illusionistic or representative ideas
- Special effect make-up

Setting

- Overall production concept
- Pre-show
- Period
- Set
- Representational/abstract/realistic
- Shown and unseen elements
- Set and set dressing
- Stage configuration
- Mood and atmosphere
- Changes in location/time/setting
- Changes in mood and atmosphere
- Impact on the audience
- Effectiveness

Director's intentions

- Production concept
- Character portrayal
- Acting style
- Choice of text
- Use of design
- Characterisation
- Proxemics
- Positioning
- Mood and atmosphere
- Choice of venue

Dramatic media

- Production concept
- Use of projection
- Use of sound
- Use of pyrotechnics
- Relationship of characters
- Interaction with technology
- Choice of colour/texture
- Layered production technology

Character development

- Production concept
- Acting style
- Status
- Relationship with other characters
- Relationship with the audience
- Mood and atmosphere
- Tension
- Interaction
- Changes in character
- Use of voice
- Use of movement
- Use of production design

 **DON'T FORGET**

You couldn't possibly cover everything in the lists and not all will apply to the performance you have seen. You only need five in-depth points for each area.

 ONLINE

To gain an understanding of how the SQA mark your essays, look at the link at www.brightredbooks.net

 ONLINE TEST

Test yourself on performance areas at www.brightredbooks.net

 ## THINGS TO DO AND THINK ABOUT

Examples are your quotations.

You will have to describe elements of the performance in order to make your points. These descriptions are your evidence that you have seen the performance (just like quotations for textual analysis essays). Look at the lists provided above and make a bulleted list of examples from the production you have seen.

PUTTING IT ALL TOGETHER

You should now have a very detailed set of notes to work from and it is time to apply your detailed understanding of the performance to an essay.

To help you tackle an essay, we will model a typical question response and how it is marked. Before we do that, there are some important points for you to remember:

1. A performance analysis essay is marked out of 20. There are 10 marks for each area.
2. A positive marking scheme is used, which means you get marks for what you include rather than deducted for what you omit – it is a friendly marking scheme, designed so that you do well!
3. You are required to choose from **four** possible performance areas and write about **two** of them.
4. You need to make **five** detailed points for each area you choose.
5. You receive one mark for each valid point and a further mark for your depth of analysis. This should include some comment on what impact the performance had on you.

HOW IS IT MARKED?

As explained above, the SQA employ a positive marking scheme. There is very clear guidance given to SQA markers and, in order to achieve the best possible marks for the performance analysis essay, it is useful to know how it is marked, as this will assist you in structuring your essay.

The first performance area you discuss, for example, setting, is referred to as 'A' by the marker. The second chosen performance area is referred to as 'B' (for example, sound). You then gain an A✓ mark for describing the acting concept used and a further A1 mark for the depth of your analysis. This is then repeated for Part B. You should create five detailed points for each performance area to achieve full marks.

Example:

> Analyse how **two** of the following have been used to illustrate the social and/or political and/or historical context of a theatrical presentation you have seen recently.
>
> • ACTING   • SETTING   • SOUND   • LIGHTING
>
> In your analysis, identify and explain in detail the ways in which your **two** selected production areas helped to communicate the social and/or political and/or historical context of the play and enhanced your appreciation of the performance.

You must give **equal weighting** to your two chosen production areas. You must give detailed analytical points to gain full marks.

Essay Plan: It is important to plan the essay and refer back to that plan throughout the writing process. It doesn't need to be detailed, just a simple list to ensure you make enough points to achieve relevant marks. Below is an example plan to tackle the question above.

> Intro – 'Kill Johnny Glendenning', Lyceum/Citz, NTS
>
> Setting
>
> 1. Contrasting sets Act 1/Act 2 to show class difference – overall production concept
> 2. Macho and manly gangster world linked to farmhouse – set
> 3. Act 2 technology – realistic set design
> 4. Performance space and pre-show
> 5. Locations – of the play and performance – changes in location

contd

Sound

1. 99 problems song – denigration of women
2. Gunshot FX – gang culture
3. Pig SFX – location and context
4. Diegetic sound throughout

As the plan shows, the student has linked his or her planned points to the example areas previously outlined. In addition to this, we can see from the simple plan where marks might be lost, as there are only four points in the plan for sound.

Part 1 – Setting: The following example paragraph identifies how the social issue of class is established through the use of setting.

> The social issue of class difference is established through the setting. Act 1 is set in a dilapidated farmhouse in Ayrshire inhabited by Auld Jim, who is an uneducated farmer. The materials used to create the set were predominantly hard and industrial-looking and there was a lot of worn wood and metal used, showing there was little comfort in the farmhouse. The second act was set in the west end of Glasgow in an upmarket apartment. Bruce, the flat's inhabitant, is educated and well-off. The apartment was very sleek, with white and cream furnishings and an opulent air. The juxtaposition of these two settings clearly shows how class and education have an effect on the comfort of one's living conditions and the opportunities that are afforded to the setting's inhabitants. This enhanced my appreciation of the performance, as the setting of Act 1 made me feel uncomfortable, whereas at curtain-up for Act 2 I felt relief as I saw there was a much more comfortable setting to contend with.

Marks are gained here for the initial description and comparison of the two sets, with an additional mark for the depth of analysis in terms of the impact on the audience and what the setting communicated.

Part 2 – Sound: The following example paragraph discusses how a particular music track was used in the production to highlight the social context of gang culture.

> Sound was also used to illustrate the play's context. The 'theme song' of the play was '99 problems' by rap artist Jay Z and this helped illustrate the social context of Glasgow gangland. Rap is often associated with gang culture, so the use of it quickly established the setting of the gang world. This creates dramatic impact, as the artist sings about rather unsettling scenarios involving violence. As an audience member, it made me guess the nature of the drama before the curtain was raised, and created tension as the play promised to be dramatic in content.

This paragraph would achieve B✓ for the initial example and the analysis of it. However, it would not achieve the B1 mark, as the point is not related clearly enough to the use of the song throughout the performance and what it added in terms of the individual's appreciation.

 THINGS TO DO AND THINK ABOUT

It is hoped that the above example clearly demonstrates how marks are allocated and how a response should be constructed. For full exemplar essays and marking guidance, see the end of this chapter.

 ONLINE

Visit www.brightredbooks.net to view marking instructions for a performance analysis essay.

 **DON'T FORGET**

Planning the essay, even briefly, focuses your thoughts and ensures you don't lose your way while writing it.

 ONLINE TEST

Test yourself on this topic at www.brightredbooks.net

EXAMPLE ESSAY — AS A DESIGNER

VIDEO LINK

Have a look at the trailer for the Old Vic's 2014 production of *The Crucible* at www.brightredbooks.net

As a designer, choose a character who is controlling or domineering. Describe **five** ways in which this control or dominance is highlighted throughout the text.

Explain in detail **five** design concepts you would use to highlight these aspects of the character to the audience.

In 'The Crucible' by Arthur Miller, the character of Abigail Williams is controlling and domineering. In this essay I will show how design concepts could be used to communicate her dominance.

In Act 1 of 'The Crucible', the audience quickly realises that Abigail is manipulating the other girls of Salem:

'… and I will bring with me a pointy reckoning that will shudder you.'

In this threat to the girls, it is understood that Abigail has a dark side to her nature and it is a turning point, as it is the first time the audience realises that she has an agenda and wants to protect herself. The audience would be shocked by this as, although they know of her affair with Proctor, it is the first time we have seen her be so upfront in her threats and need to protect herself.

As a designer, I would choose costume to help convey the idea that Abigail is set apart from the other girls and is therefore dominant over them. All the girls would wear the appropriate clothing for the time period with floor-length dresses and their heads covered with white cloth caps. Each girl's dress will be black apart from Abigail's, which would be brown in colour. This would still fit in with the Puritan society, but is slightly different from the others, which sets her apart and makes her noticeable to the audience. I would also not fix her cap to her hair with grips, so that she can remove it frequently when alone with the girls, but can put it back on when in court or with the adults of the community. This would show her rebellion and disregard for authority, and highlight how she is fearless and, therefore, able to dominate others easily.

At the end of Act 1, we encounter Abigail's first act of leading the girls – as she begins to accuse others, the girls follow her lead.

'I saw goody Sibber with the devil (it is rising to a great glee).'

Although at this point the girls are calling out the names of those who have seemingly harmed their families, it is interesting that Abigail doesn't automatically call out Elizabeth Proctor's name. This shows that she has premeditated what she is doing, as she knows she would not be believed were she to call out well-respected people's names. That had to come later once the girls are fully believed.

I would use sound and lighting design here to build the situation's tension and help elevate Abigail's status. I would use a heartbeat sound effect which would steadily speed up as the girls become more frenzied in their accusations. This would communicate the feeling of excitement the girls are feeling, most notably Abigail as she is leading the situation. I would also use a strong profile spotlight which is white to focus on Abigail as she becomes more and more gleeful in her cries. This would give her an angelic air and show how she is able to manipulate and dominate the situation, being seen as an innocent girl.

Abigail doesn't appear in Act 2 of the play although she is mentioned often. Proctor and Elizabeth argue about his contact with her:

'Elizabeth: If it were not Abigail you must go to hurt, would you falter now? I think not.'

contd

Although Abigail is not present here, it is clear that she dominates and dictates the other characters' lives and their interactions. Later in the act, Mary gives Elizabeth a doll that she has made in court while sitting beside Abigail. This again shows her controlling nature, as she has later stabbed herself in the stomach to suggest Elizabeth has done it via the doll.

To illustrate Abigail's omnipresence and control over the play's events, I would use lighting design and props. I would use a low general warm wash across the stage for the whole act, but would also have stronger-intensity orange spotlights focused on the fireplace and on the two candles on the table in the centre of the stage, to suggest firelight and candlelight. When Abigail is mentioned and discussed I would design these focused lanterns to flicker slightly, suggesting her presence and control over the other characters' lives. I would also design the poppet to resemble the actor playing Abigail, with the same hair colour and dress colour – this again would reference her presence in the scene and her controlling nature.

In Act 3, we again see Abigail's dominating nature as she leads the girls in the 'yellow bird' scene.

'Abigail and all the girls: Abby you mustn't.'

This shows how, when faced with the strength and power of Proctor and the other high-status characters onstage and in the court itself, the girls still choose to go with Abigail and follow her lead, as the wrath of the court and townspeople is not as scary as Abigail's. This clearly highlights the dominance and control she holds over the girls and the situation in Salem.

At this point, I would design my set to show the hierarchy of both the court and the girls. I would have the officials of the court, Danforth and the other judges, on a raised rostrum upstage centre, with Proctor, Giles, etc. on floor level of the stage. The girls would be situated downstage left on two benches either side of Abigail in the centre on a raised stool. This would highlight that Abigail has control over the other girls as they follow and copy her actions, and being raised up from them would illustrate this further.

In Act 4, Abigail does not appear, but the audience is made aware that she has run away from Salem with her friend Mercy Lewis.

'Thirty-one pound is gone. I am penniless.'

This highlights that although she is a dominant and controlling personality she is unable to face up to the consequences of her actions, and when it looks as if she may be punished she leaves her 'friends' and the man she loves (Proctor) to face the consequences alone. She has no redeeming features here and the audience is left with no sympathy for the character, as not only has she run out on her friends but she has also stolen from her uncle.

To highlight this to the audience I would make use of the 'Echoes down the corridor' from the end of the play. I would get the actor playing Abigail to have her photograph taken dressed as a 'prostitute in Boston'. I would project this image at the end of the play as a kind of epilogue. I would then fly in a single noose which would cast a shadow over the image of her. This would highlight how Abigail's actions and dominant nature have led to all of the horror which occurred in Salem.

 **DON'T FORGET**

The SQA employ a 'positive marking scheme' for CfE Higher Drama, which means they award marks for what you do say rather than removing marks for the omission of details.

 ONLINE TEST

See how your marking compares to the SQA's at www.brightredbooks.net

 THINGS TO DO AND THINK ABOUT

Mark this essay.

Going by what you have learned about writing essays, try marking this one. Remember, one mark is awarded for each way the character communicates the performance style, with an additional (second) mark for the depth of the response (Part A). There is one mark awarded for each appropriate acting concept, with an additional mark for the detail of the response (Part B).

 ONLINE

Have a look at further example essays online at www.brightredbooks.net

EXAMPLE ESSAY – PERFORMANCE ANALYSIS

ONLINE

The writer is discussing a very contemporary piece of theatre by the theatre company The Paper Birds. Their productions have a really strong message. Take a look at their website to find out more. You can find the link at www.brightredbooks.net

Analyse how **two** of the following have been used to represent a theatre company's message in a theatrical presentation you have seen in the recent past.

- SETTING
- ACTING
- PROPS
- SOUND

Your analysis must include details of the dramatic impact achieved and the audience's response.

I saw The Paper Birds' production of 'Broke' on 23 August 2014. In this production, The Paper Birds cleverly explored what it means to be broke and how debt affects everyone. In this essay, I will discuss how acting and setting were used in order to represent the theatre company's message.

One of the messages that the theatre company hoped to convey was that children suffer as a result of debt. This was achieved in the production through setting the play in a child's bedroom. There was a small wooden bunk bed upstage centre that only a small child would be able to fit in. There were also children's toys scattered around the set. This was powerful, as the setting of an innocent child's room, for a play exploring somewhat adult problems, put the audience in the position of the child and how they would have to go without. I empathised with the characters as a result.

> 2 marks. A strong example made clearly with insightful analysis and reference to impact on the audience.

Another message that the theatre company aimed to get across was the way debt can make people feel. The Paper Birds effectively communicated this message, using the setting, through the pre-show. When we first walked into the performance space we could see everything that was onstage, including the actors. We could already see the child's bed and the rostra set on the stage. This conveyed the message that debt can make people feel exposed and as if there is nowhere to hide.

> A✓ Although the point is clearly made it lacks detailed analysis.

Another message that The Paper Birds aimed to convey in their performance was the ways in which debt affects lifestyles. This was successfully done during the performance through the use of the rostra. There were two small black rostra which were moved several times throughout the performance in order to carry out their multiple purposes. At one point, the actors sat the rostra on their sides and used them as chairs; at another point, they used them as beds and then they were used as a till in a supermarket. The fact that these two rostra had multiple purposes throughout the performance conveyed the theatre company's message of the ways in which debt affects people's lives, as it demonstrated the idea of having to live without luxuries and make do with what they had. This helped me understand how people in debt have to 'make do' with very little.

> A✓ Clear point of multi-use set and what it conveyed.
>
> A1 Suitable depth and analysis.

Another message that the theatre company aimed to explore was the vast number and variety of people who are affected by debt. There were two large, black, telephone-box-style boxes either side of the stage which had gauze in the front of them. The actors used these boxes in order to change character, demonstrating to the audience the vast number of people who were affected by debt. This had dramatic impact as it was shocking to the audience.

> A✓ Clear point. However, the description lacks detail.

DON'T FORGET

Once you are more adept at writing these essays, you should start timing how long they take you. In the final exam you will have two hours to complete both essays.

contd

Another message that the theatre company aimed to represent through their use of setting was the number of experiences and relationships that people, including the audience, have with debt. The Paper Birds used their performance space to represent this message. The performance space was very small, with the auditorium holding roughly 40 people. This meant that the audience were in very close proximity with the actors. This made me feel connected to the actors and the stories they were telling. The performance space was extremely hot and stuffy. This atmosphere imitated the stress that debt can cause and made the audience feel stressed and flustered and successfully represented the message of the theatre company.

> A✓ & A1 Clear link between the setting and the performance environment and its connection to it.

The Paper Birds also conveyed their message that children suffer as a result of debt through their acting. Jemma McDonnell did this by playing a young child at one point in the performance. She used a high-pitched voice and lively gestures and body language to create a believable child-like character. She also held a personal prop of a teddy bear. This had dramatic impact as I felt sympathetic towards this character, as I knew that debt and money problems had affected the way this child would live her life.

> A✓ Clear explanation of the acting point, but lacks analysis.

The Paper Birds also aimed to convey the message that politics may affect people's debt and their relationship with money. They used their acting to do this as they used sock puppets and did puppetry. They explored the political effects of debt by acting out a House of Commons debate using sock puppets. This has a comical effect as the audience thought of politicians as puppets.

> No marks. This isn't a fully made point.

The Paper Birds also aim to convey the message of the negative effects that debt can have on people. In a speech at the end, Jemma McDonnell used quick twitchy gestures and closed-up body language to show how much stress debt has caused Sally. She also used a worried and anxious tone and a quiet volume to show how much debt had affected Sally. This had dramatic impact as I was worried about the real Sally due to the verbatim nature of the performance.

> A✓ & A1 Clear analysis and details of the effect on the audience.

Another message that the theatre company hoped to convey was that debt affects everyone, including the audience members. The actors sometimes spoke directly to the audience and broke character; for example, the male actor said to an audience member, 'We need to move the projector'. This made the audience feel included in the performance. They also, each in turn, spoke of their own experience of debt as they broke character and spoke as themselves. This was hugely effective and made the audience think about their own experience of debt and relationship with money. This made me consider how debt affected me and how I may have been sheltered from it by my own parents.

> A✓ & A1 This is a very clear point and the analysis is very good.

The Paper Birds also aimed to convey the message that there are a vast number and range of people who are affected by debt by using multi-role. Jemma McDonnell played the character Sally. She also played the character of an older man who was very middle-class and had been affected by debt. The contrast between these two characters showed the vast range of people who have been affected by debt. In order to portray this male character, Jemma altered her body language and posture to make it more man-like and used a deeper pitch of voice. This shocked the audience as they did not expect a man from a middle-class background to have been so severely affected by debt and to have such a bad relationship with money.

> No marks. This is a good point well made. However, the writer has only analysed the work of one actor in the production. To describe and analyse the acting in a performance, you must provide in-depth information on a range of performances.

In conclusion, The Paper Birds aimed to communicate several messages in their performances of 'Broke'. They used both acting and setting very skilfully in order to do this.

> This essay would receive 13/20, which is a fair response. It is pretty clear where marks have been lost in terms of lack of detail or repetition.

 ## THINGS TO DO AND THINK ABOUT

Could you improve on this essay?

Using this essay as a model, write your own version for a performance you have seen recently.

COURSE ASSESSMENT

CHOOSING YOUR ROLE

Higher Drama is different from National 4 and National 5 in that it is entirely externally assessed. This means that the written exam will be marked by SQA markers and rigorously checked and verified. The practical exam will be marked by a visiting assessor (VA). All of the VAs and paper markers are drama teachers themselves, or recently retired drama teachers. They have undergone training and there are a number of levels of quality assurance in place to ensure your exams are marked fairly. A positive marking scheme is employed across the course, which means you do not 'lose' marks by missing things out or making inaccurate points, but you are awarded marks for the correct points you make.

HOW TO CHOOSE YOUR ROLE

For the practical exam, you have the choice of three specialisms: acting, directing or design. Over the course, you will have gained an awareness of where your strengths lie and areas where you perhaps need support. You will be assisted in making your choice and it is important to prioritise and weigh up your options carefully in order to make the correct decision. Enjoyment should be a factor when choosing your role – it can be very difficult to focus and develop your skills in a particular area if you are bored witless by it! However, it is also essential that you are able to establish the area in which you will succeed and, in the end, receive the best possible grade. During the Production Skills unit, you will have gained a fair idea of what is required within each role. However, for the final exam you specialise in a single area and the requirements are an extended version of what you have done previously.

WEIGHING UP YOUR OPTIONS

The following is an overview of what is required in each role. It is important that, when you make the decision to specialise in a specific area, you are fully aware of the requirements of the role and how it is marked.

Acting

If you choose to specialise in acting for the performance exam, you will be required to prepare two acting roles. Each role must involve interaction with at least one other character (who may or may not be assessed in this role). Each acting piece should be a maximum of ten minutes long. You are marked by a VA. Each aspect of the performance is worth 5 marks, with each role being marked from a total of 25.

- **Understanding** – Communicating the agreed interpretation of acting concepts by demonstrating an understanding of character through the use of textual clues.

- **Portrayal** – Sustaining character and conveying relationships through credible interaction with other characters.

- **Voice** – Appropriate and effective use of voice.

- **Movement** – Appropriate and effective use of movement.

- **Impact** – Impact on audience.

Broadly speaking, each aspect of the performance is marked on a range of 'unconvincing' to 'excellent'.

contd

Directing

For the directing option, you will prepare to direct an act from your chosen text. On the day of the exam the VA will choose two consecutive pages, which you will be given time to prepare, before being observed conducting a rehearsal of these pages. Each aspect of your direction will be marked from 10, with the total marks available for the practical assessment in directing being 50.

- **Understanding** – Setting the extract in the context of the whole play and communicating directorial concepts, including establishing characterisation.

- **Movement** – Directing the use of movement and considering stage proxemics within the blocking process to communicate aspects of the plot, themes and issues contained in the extract, and the development of characterisation and relationships.

- **Voice** – Directing the use of voice, including delivery of lines to communicate aspects of the plot, themes and issues contained in the extract, and the development of characterisation and relationships.

- **Interaction** – Interaction, engagement and responsiveness throughout the process.

- **Impact** – Directorial impact when showing the final run-through of the extract.

In broad terms, each aspect of direction is marked on a range of 'little direction' to 'excellent direction'.

Design

For the design specialism, you will prepare designs for the whole of your chosen text. You will specialise in two areas, the first being set design which is worth 30 marks. You can choose one of the following production areas: lighting, sound, props, costume, or make-up and hair. Your second production area must complement your set design and is worth 20 marks. There are also 10 marks available for the Preparation for Performance.

- **Design concept** – In response to the chosen text, producing creative and effective design concepts in relation to requirements of the drama and needs of the actors.

- **Ground plans** – Producing working and final ground plans for the specified performance space, including elevations, with reference to textual clues.

- **Ideas development** – Development of ideas from initial thoughts, designs and research to final design concept.

- **Additional production role** – Responding to text to produce creative and effective notes/plotting sheets/plans/designs/drawings in relation to additional role.

- **Additional production role** – Demonstrating practical skills in relation to additional role: either by demonstration of lighting states or sound effects, or with one made prop or one made costume, or application of one make-up and hair.

Broadly speaking, marks are awarded on a range of 'unconvincing' to 'full and detailed'.

 THINGS TO DO AND THINK ABOUT

Look at the requirements for each role and your performance in the previous two units. If it isn't clear which role you should undertake, you can make a pros and cons list to weigh up your options. This list should reflect your experiences, abilities and preferences. Following this and through discussions with your teacher/lecturer and peers, you should be able to make an informed choice.

 DON'T FORGET

Whichever role you assume for the final assessment, you must be organised and use your time wisely in order to prepare for the final performance and assessment.

ONLINE

To find out more about how the three roles work in a professional theatre production, look at www.brightredbooks.net

ONLINE TEST

Test yourself online at www.brightredbooks.net

THE PROCESS

In this section, we will examine the requirements of each role in more detail and look at possible activities which should help you reach the required standard to achieve your full potential in the final exam. You can look back at the production role chapter for guidance on what activities you can carry out to help develop your work. The following is an overview of the process for each role using the familiar stages of initial, refined and final concepts.

ACTING

For this specialism, you need to play two roles. They don't have to be contrasting, but should show off the range of your abilities. Here are some guidelines for approaching these roles and generating evidence to draw from when putting together your Preparation for Performance.

Initial ideas – You should begin to develop your interpretation of each character. This should be informed by your understanding of the character's journey throughout the whole play and from research conducted into the historical, social and **political context** of the play. You may be involved in workshopping and improvisation during this stage of the process, in addition to individual research and development tasks.

Refined ideas – At this point, you should be blocking the extract and developing your use of voice, movement and characterisation. There are a number of activities you may be involved in during this stage, but primarily these will be practical. You need to use time out of rehearsal to learn your lines and cues, and to develop your character further.

Final ideas – In the later stages of rehearsal, you should be refining and honing all of your ideas and development in order to create a fully rounded character. You may also be using props and costume to help enhance your character, but these should be used sparingly as the focus must be on how you illustrate the character rather than on your use of props and costume.

DON'T FORGET

The SQA allow you to use props and costume in the assessed performance, but only those required for specific business, or essential movement.

DIRECTING

You will be required to conduct a rehearsal of a scene of around two pages (selected by the VA). This rehearsal should be seen as the first rehearsal of the section; it should be planned and clearly demonstrate your knowledge of the context of the whole play.

Initial ideas – You should be planning and researching the text, and beginning to make decisions about the setting of the play. You should take notes and make rough plans about what you wish to achieve through your direction.

Refined – In the development process, you should split your chosen act/section into 'actions'. This will break down the text into more manageable chunks and allow you to approach each one. You should plan the blocking for the whole act and workshop your ideas for each action to check if they work and link together coherently.

contd

Final – Upon blocking the whole act/section, you should have experience of how to go about structuring a rehearsal. Broadly speaking, this should be broken down into the following sections:

- **Exposition** – Explaining to your actors the thoughts behind the forthcoming rehearsal; this should reflect your knowledge of the play and its context and how you view the characters and their relationships.

- **Warm-up** – Choose an activity or improvisation which works towards the aims of the rehearsal.

- **Blocking** – You should work with your actors to block the action or extract in line with your plans, fully justifying your ideas and being mindful of what the actors bring to the role.

- **De-brief** – Chat with your actors about what has been achieved in the rehearsal and evaluate both your and their performance in it. Plan your next steps.

If you use this model to block the whole act and follow a similar format for every workshop or rehearsal, you will be fully prepared with exercises and ideas to conduct your rehearsal in front of the VA.

DESIGN

Initial – Informed by extensive research, you should begin to develop your ideas for set and staging. You design for the whole play, so you must know it inside out and back to front! You should be generating sketches, ground plans and mood boards to gain a full picture of what you want to achieve from your design.

Refined – At this stage, your ideas should be beginning to take shape. The set design can be conceptual (you don't have to actually build it, just illustrate what you wish to achieve and how you will do this). Creating a 'rehearsal set' is useful at this point, in addition to elevation and scale drawings and perhaps even a set model. You should also be developing your ideas for the second production area (see production roles chapter for guidance on this, pages 28–56).

Final – You should be creating final drawings, models and plans at this point. In addition, you should be developing and applying your concepts for the second area: making the prop or costume, practising make-up application and creating make-up plans, or experimenting and choosing lighting states/sounds and creating cue sheets. At this stage, you should also be rehearsing how you will present your ideas to the VA and deciding how to display your created designs.

 THINGS TO DO AND THINK ABOUT

Begin to work through the processes above, ensuring you keep a logbook or diary as you go, which will help create a bank of materials to reference when writing the Preparation for Performance.

 **DON'T FORGET**

The set design is conceptual, but you need to apply skills to the second production area.

 ONLINE

Find the SQA assessment specification at www.brightredbooks.net

 ONLINE TEST

Head to www.brightredbooks.net and take the topic test.

PREPARATION FOR PERFORMANCE

WHAT IS THE PFP?

The Preparation for Performance is a document which you write, and it is marked by the visiting assessor (VA) before your practical exam. The idea is that you can communicate your process to the examiner to give them an understanding of how you reached your performance concepts. It is not a folio or extended piece of writing, but an overview of the work you have undertaken and what they can expect to see in performance.

> **Before anything else, preparation is the key to success.**
>
> *Alexander Graham Bell*

The PfP should be around 500 words.

It constitutes 10 of the 60 marks available for the performance component of the course.

It should provide information about:

- research into the chosen text(s)
- interpretation of the chosen role
- process (development and progression) of acting or directing or design concept.

If you are performing as a director or designer, you should discuss the text you have been developing from. If you are performing as an actor, you will discuss both roles. The following examples should help you see how to structure the PfP to fit into the given criteria.

How is it marked?

The VA will mark all of the PfPs on the day of the exam. This will happen before any of the performances have taken place. The PfP is marked holistically and responses fall into the following categories.

Full and detailed (9–10 marks):
- a detailed description of the research
- insight into the historical, social and political context
- a description of the chosen role
- reflects a range of thoughts and ideas for the specialism relating to the research etc.
- a full account of the development

Fairly detailed (7–8 marks):
- a description of the research
- some insight into the historical, social and political context
- a description of the chosen role
- reflects thoughts and ideas for the specialism relating to the research etc.
- an account of the development

Basic account (5–6 marks):
- a description of some research
- adequate knowledge of the historical, social and political context
- a simple description of the chosen role
- reflects a few thoughts and ideas for the specialism relating to the research etc.
- a simple description of the development

DON'T FORGET

You don't need to name the play in an introduction; this information is already there.

contd

Limited account (3–4 marks):
- a limited description of some research
- some knowledge of the historical, social and political context
- a simple description of the chosen role
- reflects one or two thoughts and ideas for the specialism relating to the research etc.
- a limited description of the development

Weak account (1–2 marks):
- refers to some research
- little reference to the historical, social and political context
- a limited description of the chosen role
- little or no reflection of thoughts relating to specialism for the specialism relating to the research etc.
- little or no details of the process

No evidence (0 marks).

The example given below is designed to help you understand how to structure a Preparation for Performance from the perspective of a director.

Example:

Director

Initially, I researched the time period of the play and the allegorical time period of the 1950s. I also looked at different productions of it and there were so many that I had to narrow my focus, as there was actually too much information and I didn't know where to start. I used the internet, SparkNotes and study guides as well as the film 'Goodnight and Good Luck' to research the context of the play. I found that Miller himself was brought before the HUAA and many of his contemporaries were accused of being communists, just like in 1692 Salem. I wanted to clearly communicate the issues of McCarthyism which permeate Miller's text and so found some archive footage from the period which I felt I may be able to use to echo the words of Danforth. I also had the idea to get the actor playing him to take on some of Senator McCarthy's vocal inflections to reflect Miller's life experiences. I broke the act down into actions to isolate sections and moments. I then created a rehearsal schedule and blocked each action on the text, before trying it out with actors and checking it worked before moving on to the next action. I feel, as a director, it is my job to interpret the text well and communicate this through the action onstage. There are many complexities to the characters and relationships and so I did a lot of character work and improvisation with the actors to shape the action of the act. I also gave my cast information about the character they were playing and the context of the play to help them develop their characters. My original concept to link the two time periods in my portrayal should be achieved through my use of the archive footage. As the act takes place in a courtroom, I researched images of courtrooms both current and historical, and used this to inform the positioning of my characters, for example, Danforth on a high rostrum, with the girls, like a jury, sitting on benches to his left. The courtroom setting can be challenging in that it can restrict movement. To combat this I had Danforth come down from his platform early on and use proxemics to threaten and challenge the other characters when needed. As the piece developed, it was easy to develop my concepts and link the two situations.

 VIDEO LINK

To hear from the director of the Young Vic's production of *The Crucible* (2015) and find out her directing concepts, head to www.brightredbooks.net

 THINGS TO DO AND THINK ABOUT

Compare the example PfP with the bulleted guide above it. Imagine you are a visiting assessor and consider which category you feel it best fits into. NB: if you feel it is between two categories, award the highest associated mark – so, if it is between 'limited' and 'weak' it would achieve a value of 3, according to the positive marking scheme applied to Higher Drama.

 ONLINE TEST

Head to www.brightredbooks.net and test yourself on this topic.

THE DAY OF THE PRACTICAL EXAM

The practical assessment will most likely take place on a single day, depending on the number of people being assessed. It can be a long, challenging, but ultimately rewarding, experience and many even enjoy it! The practical assessment is a closed exam, which means a small, suitable and sympathetic audience will be in attendance, at the arrangement of your school or college. This removes the added pressure of performing in front of friends and loved ones, as this may weaken your performance. The following is an outline of a typical exam day, with some advice on presenting your work and combating your nerves.

Your teacher or lecturer will have agreed an agenda for the assessment day. Usually, the VA will introduce themself upon arrival and put everyone at ease with some informal advice. The VA will then take some time privately to mark the PfPs. Following this, the VA will usually assess the directors and designers first (before the audience arrives); they will then watch and assess the actors one after the other. Between each assessment piece the VA will need some time to take notes and write down their marking for each candidate. All Higher Drama students are assessed immediately after the performance to ensure the impact of it is not lost, and to avoid any confusion.

MANAGING YOUR NERVES

It is natural to feel nervous before your practical assessment, and nerves show you care about succeeding. They also can help energise you for the performance or presentation. It is important that you manage your nerves so that they don't hinder your performance. Whichever role you are undertaking in the practical assessment, there is an element of presentation, whether acting your roles, or the presentation to the VA. The following simple techniques can be used to help with your nerves:

- **Rehearse** – This seems obvious advice for actors, but it is important that you know every aspect of the performance really well. If you are a designer, you must rehearse what you are going to say during the presentation and you should always rehearse in front of others. If you are a director, you should workshop all of the scenes/pages in the act before the exam so that you have a clear idea of what you will do on the day itself.

ONLINE

More advice on coping with nerves can be found at www.brightredbooks.net

DON'T FORGET

All VAs are drama teachers. They have students going through the same process as you and they understand exactly how you feel!

contd

- **Remember to breathe** – Adrenalin causes our breathing to become shallow; taking deep breaths tricks the body into thinking we are calm.

- **Smile** – Smiling makes us feel happier and calmer.

- **Pause** – Take a moment to collect your thoughts before you start the performance/presentation.

- **Slow down** – Speak at a slower pace than you would in everyday conversation. This will assist you in controlling your breathing and pausing.

- **Enjoy it!** – This may seem unlikely, but once you are in the flow you should be able to start enjoying the experience!

Downtime

There will be considerable periods of time when you are not needed onstage but will be expected to become part of the audience. You must try to be as encouraging and as gracious about others' performances as possible. If you have a short gap between your own acting pieces, you should grab a few minutes to refocus yourself and think about the next character you are going to portray. If you have carried out your design presentation or directed your rehearsal, you may well be involved in helping your actors in some way, by using your technical skills, or reading-in for others' acting pieces, or prompting.

Reading-in is necessary in the assessment as, unfortunately, not every play is written with equally weighted parts. If you are required to read-in for another cast member, it is important that you are helpful and generous, but not at the expense of your own examined pieces. It is not an SQA requirement that you learn the lines for a read-in, but it is advisable to do so, in order that the actors being examined have more to react to and are not impeded, in terms of any business or eye contact, by you holding the text.

For technical support, the SQA advise that lighting and sound should be used if available, and if required by the extract being performed. They should not detract from the performance, however, and should be simple and straightforward. In terms of lighting, a general wash is usually enough, with a **fade up** or **down** at the beginning and end of the performance. Music should not be played between performances, but can be used if specified in the text. The same rule applies to sound effects.

 ## THINGS TO DO AND THINK ABOUT

Throughout the course, you will have become close to your peers in drama. The practical assessment day is a time when you can show off what you have learned and support each other to succeed. Discuss and make a plan so that the workload is shared equally and it isn't the same person doing everything. Once you have decided who will do which thing for each performance, make sure you rehearse with the required people in good time before the assessment day so that everything runs smoothly in the performance.

 ONLINE TEST

Head to www.brightredbooks.net and test yourself on this topic.

THE WRITTEN EXAM

The written exam is worth 40 marks. It has two parts, both of which require you to write an essay (worth 20 marks each). The exam papers are marked by SQA-appointed markers and are verified and checked stringently by the SQA. The following section looks at how you should approach the written exam.

WHY A WRITTEN EXAM?

Drama is usually taught as a fairly practical subject; with a focus on creating and performance. However, there is another important side to drama and theatre, and this must be reflected in the assessment for Higher Drama. To understand a theatre text and to appreciate live performance is an essential skill, especially if you move on to study drama or theatre in the future. Drama is an academic subject (regardless of its image) and the written exam is necessary to assess and quantify that.

APPROACHING THE EXAM

Structure

The Higher Drama exam is split into two parts. Part A covers textual analysis and Part B covers performance analysis. Over the duration of the course, you will have gained a great deal of experience writing essays and this should shine through in the written exam. However, the added pressure here is the time aspect. The time limit for the exam is two hours, which allows you less than an hour to write each essay, as you should allow time for reading and choosing the question in Part A, as well as checking your work and adding to the essays if necessary. There is a choice of questions in Part A, which covers the three specialisms of acting, directing and design. You do not need to respond to the questions from the perspective of the role you have undertaken for the practical assessment: for example, you can direct for the practical assessment and answer an 'as an actor' question in the written paper. In Part B, there is a single question which you must answer using two production areas (from a choice of four).

Choosing the question

It is easy and natural to have a preconceived idea of which type of essay question you could tackle. However, as there is no way to predict exactly what will come up in the written paper, it is important that you are prepared to answer any of the possible questions which could appear. First of all, you must read the questions carefully; if there is any word or aspect of the question you don't fully understand, this question is probably not the best one to approach. Choose the question you feel most confident about, not necessarily the one that most closely reflects your preferences. Once you have chosen the most appropriate question, you can proceed with formulating your response.

contd

DON'T FORGET

You don't need to write about the same area you have undertaken for the practical assessment.

Managing your time in the exam

You should use the same process to approach the essays in both Part A and Part B of the exam paper. The following steps can be used as a model for tackling the written exam and managing your time effectively.

1 Note down a timeline. This will help you manage your time and plan your essays quickly. The timeline may not be split 50/50, in terms of time for each essay, as it may be that you are able to write performance analysis essays more quickly than textual analysis, or vice versa. This is personal to you and reflects your own skills and abilities. It may look something like the example below.

Example:

9:00 – read entire paper

9:05 – reread Part A and choose question

9:10 – plan Part A

9:15 – write Part A

10:00 – reread and plan Part B

10:10 – write Part B

10:50 – read over answers and add any missed points

2 Write a plan. Writing a plan for your essays will help ensure you structure the essays properly and cover all the relevant points. This doesn't need to be detailed but should be enough to jog your memory, make the appropriate points and, in the case of Part A, remind you of textual references and plot points.

3 Write the essay.

4 Read over your answer and check you have made the correct number of points and referenced the appropriate textual/performance examples.

5 Repeat the process for the second essay.

6 Read over both answers and add any points you may have missed.

ONLINE

There are past and specimen exam papers online, together with marking instructions, at www.brightredbooks.net

 THINGS TO DO AND THINK ABOUT

During your revision, you should practise writing essays within the allotted time frame. This will help you get used to what is expected in the final exam, and to become more familiar with the process and problems you may encounter. Try to write as many essays in response to questions you don't like as to ones you do. You don't know if your favoured essay type will appear in the final exam and you need to be prepared in case it doesn't.

 ONLINE TEST

Test yourself on this topic at www.brightredbooks.net

APPENDICES

GLOSSARY OF TERMS

DRAMA SKILLS

Action
Events of a drama

Amateur
A person who works in the theatre for pleasure and not for money

Audience
People watching a performance

Audition
Practical 'interview' for an acting role

Auditorium
Seating area for the audience

Character
Part which an actor plays

Communicate
Tell, put across

Contribute
Offer ideas, input into a drama

Cue
Signal for something to happen

Dialogue
Speech between characters

Drama process
The process of creating a drama from stimulus

Dramatic irony
When something is understood by the audience, but not the characters

Develop
Make more detailed

Episodic
Of a drama that is linked by a theme rather than a storyline

Evaluate
Assess and offer next steps

Experiment
Try out

Focus
Central point/main character/relationship/event/issue

Given circumstances
Facts about a character/situation which don't change

Key moment
Important point in the drama

Language
The words used in the drama

Lines
Written text which actors speak

Location
Where the drama is set

Message
The overall point communicated

Mood/atmosphere
The intended feeling created by the performance within the audience

Performance
The presentation of a drama

Playwright
The author of a play

Plot
The central action around which the play is written

Plot twist
When the action takes an unexpected turn

Portrayal
How a character is shown by an actor

Purpose
The intention of the drama or character – what they are there to do

Reaction
Response to what has happened

Realistic
Believable, like real life

Rehearsal
Practising in the run-up to a performance

Scenario
Outline of the drama's plot

Scene
Part of a drama set in one place and time

Script
Written words of a drama – lines and stage directions

Status
The importance of a character in relation to others

Stimulus
The starting point of any drama

Storyline
The overall events of the drama

Target audience
Who the drama will be best performed to

Tension
The driving force of any drama

Time period
When the drama happens

Venue
The place where the performance takes place

Movement

Balance
Even distribution of weight

Body language
Unspoken communication

contd

Eye contact
Looking at another character or the audience directly

Facial expression
Look on face that shows emotion

Gesture
Meaningful movement, usually of the hand or head

Levels
Height position of the body

Mannerism
Habit of gesture

Movement
Physical expression

Naturalistic
Of movement that is natural

Pace
Speed of voice or movement

Positioning
Placement on stage

Posture
Position of the body, how it is held

Rhythm
Moving to a beat

Timing
Moving at the correct point

Voice

Accent
Way of speaking in a local area

Articulation
Clear and distinct speech

Clarity
Clearness of voice, being heard and understood

Diction
Clear pronunciation and clarity

Emphasis
Stress put on a word or phrase

Fluency
Clear, fluid speech

Intonation
The rising and falling of the voice

Pace
Speed of speech

Pause
Break in speaking, short silence

Pitch
How high/low the voice is

Register
Way of speaking appropriately to the person being spoken to

Tone
Use of voice to express emotion

Form/genre/style

Agitprop
A political play

Allegory
A symbolic narrative in which the surface details imply a secondary meaning

Comedy
A funny play

Comedy of manners
Comedic play using societal references recognised by the audience

Commedia dell'arte
Drama using stock characters and scenarios in improvised touring theatre

Dance drama
A drama told using dance moves

Docudrama
A recreation of actual events

Farce
A comical, exaggerated drama

Forum theatre
Drama which involves the audience in affecting the outcome

Historical drama
A play set in a particular historical setting

Melodrama
An exaggerated drama with over-the-top characters and unlikely scenarios

Mime
Stylised movement, creating the illusion of reality (no speech)

Monologue
A play in which only one person speaks

Musical
A play using music or song and dance

Pantomime
A traditional British comedy performance, with its own conventions

Parody
Comical (mocking) imitation

Physical theatre
Drama using physical movement to tell a story

Play scripted or improvised
A rehearsed play created from a text or developed through improvisation

Satire
A play which reflects and makes comment on a familiar situation

Tragedy
A play with an unhappy ending

Tragi-comedy
Sad play with comical elements

contd

GLOSSARY OF TERMS (Contd.)

Verbatim
Using the words of real people as a play's dialogue

Conventions

Aside
Comment made directly to the audience

Dialogue
Conversation between two or more characters

Flashback
A scene showing an earlier event

Flashforward
A scene showing a later event

Freeze frame
A short freeze which marks the moment before the action continues

Narration
Telling all or part of the story

Slow motion
When everything moves at an exaggerated slow pace

Soliloquy
A lengthy speech presented alone on stage

Split stage/focus
The action alternates between two sides of the acting area

Tableau
A frozen image that tells a story

Voiceover
A recorded speech that can comment upon or narrate the action

Characterisation techniques

Character iceberg
A pictorial representation of the inner and outer character persona

Character profile/cards
A detailed description of a character

Giving witness/reportage
Reporting on unseen events

Hot seating
Questioning a character in role

Improvisation
Creating without a script or plan

Mantle of the expert
The actor is an expert on a specific subject and improvises as if they know everything about it

Role on the wall
Facts and assumptions noted down around the character's outline

Role play
Taking on the attitudes/beliefs of a character

Role reversal
Actors swapping roles to enhance understanding

Thought tracking
The character speaking his or her thoughts aloud

Thought tunnel
Characters commenting on a situation until a decision is made

Voices in the head
Recalled voices are heard or the audience hear the character's thoughts (for example, angel/devil)

Writing in role
Writing in the first person as a character

Structure and style

Antagonist
A character or force against which another character struggles

Climax
The turning point of the action in the plot of a play or story; the climax represents the point of greatest tension in the work

Comic relief
The use of a comic scene to interrupt a succession of intensely tragic dramatic moments

Complication
An intensification of the conflict in a story or play

Conflict
A struggle between opposing forces in performance

Denouement
The resolution of the plot

Exposition
The first stage of a dramatic plot

Falling action
In the plot of a play, the action following the climax of the work that moves it towards its denouement or resolution

Foil
A character who contrasts and parallels the main character in a play

Foreshadowing
Hints of what is to come in the action

Linear
A chronological order of scenes

Non-linear
A drama that shifts in time through use of flashbacks/flashforwards

Protagonist
The main character of a drama

contd

Recognition
The point at which a character understands his or her situation as it really is

Resolution
The sorting out or unravelling of a plot at the end of a play

Reversal
The point at which the action of the plot turns in an unexpected direction for the protagonist

Rising action
A set of conflicts leading up to the climax of the plot

Subject
What a story or play is about

Subplot
A subsidiary or subordinate or parallel plot in a play

Symbol
An object or action that stands for something beyond itself

PRODUCTION SKILLS

Catharsis
The purging of the feelings of pity and fear that occur in the audience of a tragic drama

Central metaphor
A recurring or common image

Chorus
A group of characters in Greek theatre who comment on the action of a play without participating in it

Connotation
The use of words, symbols, etc. to communicate wider issues or themes

Contrasts
How aspects of the plot/production contrast to communicate meaning

Design concept
An idea for design which can be developed and used in a performance

Dramatis personae
Latin for the characters or persons in a play

Figurative language
A form of language use in which writers and speakers convey something other than the literal meaning of their words

Fourth wall
The imaginary wall of proscenium arch or end-on staging

Historical context
Where and when the play is set and the situation at this time

Illusionistic setting or stylised setting
Design/setting that is not literal

Imagery
The pattern of related details in a performance

Message
What the play/company/director/designer is trying to communicate

Pathos
Quality of a play's action that stimulates the audience to feel pity for a character

Performance concept
Idea for performance as an actor, director or designer

Personification
The endowment of inanimate objects or abstract concepts with animate or living qualities

Plot
The story

Political context
The political situation at the time the play was written/set

Period
Era/time setting

Pre-show
Everything that happens before the official start of the play, usually as the audience enter

Production concept
Ideas developed and delivered in performance relating to a specific production area

Scenic directions
Explanations at the beginning of a play that provide details of the setting

Setting
The time and place that establish a play's context

Social context
The social situation of the time the play was written/set

Stage direction
Notes in text that offer the actor/director/designer information

Staging
The spectacle a play presents in performance

Subject
The model for make-up/costume application

Tragic flaw
A weakness or limitation of a character

contd

GLOSSARY OF TERMS (Contd.)

Tragic hero
A privileged, exalted character of high repute, who, by virtue of a tragic flaw and fate, suffers a fall from glory into suffering

Visual images
Projections, scenic design, tableaux, proxemics

Acting

Actor–audience relationship
Connection between the actors and the audience

Characterisation
The process of developing a character

Ensemble
Group of actors, often taking on several small roles in the performance

Innovation/creativity
Originality of acting/production techniques

Interaction
How the characters communicate with each other

Mood, atmosphere and tension
Created through production and acting techniques

Movement
Balance, body language, mannerism, stance, gesture, levels, eye contact, naturalistic, stylised, rhythm, timing

Multi-role
When the same actor plays a number of characters

Relationship of text and physicality
How the text informs the physical actions onstage

Voice
Tone, pitch, emphasis, accent, diction, clarity, volume, register, dialect, projection, articulation, emphasis, pause, pace

Set/Staging

Backdrop
Curtain across the back of the stage, often depicting a particular scene

Backstage
Any area of the theatre where actors/crew prepare for a performance

Cyclorama
A white cloth which can be lit and projected on to

Flats
Wooden frames covered in canvas, can be painted

Flies
Area above the stage where scenery is flown in from

Rake
Slope of stage or seating

Revolve
A stage or part of a stage that turns

Rostrum (plural rostra)
Blocks/platforms used to create levels

Stage configuration
End-on, proscenium arch, traverse, thrust, promenade, site-specific, immersive

Trucks
Set which is on wheels and can be easily manipulated

Vomitorium
Entrance/exit passages/corridors for the audience in a theatre

Props

Costume prop
A prop which is worn and used by a character (for example, glasses)

Personal prop
A prop which is brought onstage and used by a character

Props table
An area clearly labelled and used to store props

Set prop
A prop placed on the set

Lighting

B/O
Blackout, no light onstage

Blacklight
A fluorescent light which highlights white and neon colours

Barn doors
Flaps that can be adjusted to alter the beam

Channel
The dimmer (slider) allocated to each light

Crossfade
The change from one lighting state to another without a blackout in between

Fade up/down
To brighten or fade the light (fast or slow)

Flood
Lantern creating a wide light spread

Focus
Positioning of lights on the rig/bar

Follow spot
Spotlight which can follow the action

Fresnel
Lantern creating a soft-edged beam of light

Gel
Film placed over lantern to create colour

contd

Gobo
Metal plate with cut-out shape or pattern

Intensity/level
How bright the light will be (usually 1–10 scale)

Key light
Light from an obvious source (window/candle)

Parcan
A lantern used to reflect strong colours onto the acting area

Profile
A lantern giving a hard-edged beam of light

Strobe
A light which flashes on and off at a regular speed

Timing
Snap to/crossfade

Wash
The whole acting area is evenly lit

Sound

Crossfade
The change from one cue to another, no silence in between

Fade up/down
To increase/decrease the volume

Foley SFX
Sound effect created using various items (for example, coconut shells for horse approaching)

Live SFX
SFX created live

Pre-recorded
SFX are recorded and played in the performance

Snap to
Silence is achieved instantly

Volume/level
Level of sound: low, medium, high (numerical level of slider 10)

Costume

Accessories
Hats, gloves, ribbons, hairbands, glasses, handbags, fans, jewellery, etc.

Adapted costume
An item which is sourced and then altered or embellished

Colour matching
Choosing complementary shades for characters who are connected

Period costume
Clothing appropriate to a given time period

Specials
Fat suits, pregnancy bumps, hooped skirts, shoulder pads, etc.

Stylised/representational costume
Costume which is designed to be symbolic in some way

Tailoring
The shape and fit of clothing

Make-up and hair

Crepe hair
Plaits of artificial hair which can be cut and trimmed to form eyebrows, moustaches and beards

Derma wax
Hard wax which becomes malleable when worked; used for scarring, noses, etc.

Fake blood
Powder, liquid or capsules which create the effect of bleeding

Foundation
The base coat applied to the face which is the basic skin colour

Highlighting
Using light colours to make areas of the face stand out

Latex
Rubber that can be used to make a skull cap, moulds or false noses

Liners
Sticks of make-up in different colours used to create lines, bruises, shading, highlighting, etc.

Liquid latex
Used to create scars

Nose putty
Type of clay used for altering the shape of the nose or chin

Pencils
Soft pencils in different colours which are easily smudged and blended

Scarring
Scars created with make-up, putty or scarring material

Shading
Using colours to make areas of the face look shrunken

Spirit gum
Glue used to attach hair to the face

Stipple sponge
Used to create unshaven look or the appearance of cracked veins

Tooth varnish
Used to create the look of a missing tooth by blacking out the existing one